THE EARTH
FROM THE AIR

Yann Arthus-Bertrand

THE EARTH
FROM THE AIR

Thames & Hudson

For Anne, Tom, Guillaume and Baptiste.
With love.

*This vision of the world could not have been possible without
the aid of UNESCO, Fujifilm, Corbis and Air France.
I am grateful for their confidence and friendship.*

Translated from the French *La terre vue du ciel* by David Baker

First published in the United Kingdom in 1999 by
Thames & Hudson Ltd, 181A High Holborn, London WC1V 7QX

Reprinted in 1999, 2000, 2001

© 1999 Thames & Hudson Ltd, London and Harry N. Abrams, Inc., New York

Original Edition © 1999 Éditions de la Martinière, Paris, France

British Library Cataloguing-in-Publication Data
A catalogue record for this book is available from the British Library

ISBN 0-500-01955-X

Printed and bound in France

Yann Arthus-Bertrand has accompanied me throughout my twenty years as a publisher. In 1979 I published his first book at Hachette Réalités. He and his wife, Anne, had just returned from Kenya, where they had lived for two years, and his photographs of lions caused a sensation. Since then, not a year has passed without our publishing one or more books together. I have watched this tireless and talented photographer develop, as he continually crisscrossed the globe in search of humankind—and himself.

Earth from Above represents the end of a journey to which Yann has devoted so much of himself. Ten years of work, hundreds of thousands of miles traveled and photographs taken, stepping out of one airplane and into another, from one country to another, playing with time zones. But all of this would amount to nothing if it were not for his incomparable eye: an eye that always finds the detail to make a photograph more beautiful, an eye that understands and investigates people and places.

This book is not simply a series of pictures. It is the testimony of a citizen of the world at the dawn of the third millennium, who is eager to show his vision of the earth, its beauty as well as its failures. His enthusiasm is coupled with a concern about the transformation of this planet. The texts that accompany these dazzling photographs are a necessary counterpoint, offering an inventory of the earth today.

But the book is not an end in itself. In fact, it is just a beginning. Yann will continue to enrich his record of the world until he leaves it. Who knows, perhaps he will then begin to photograph the next world—a project that he will have eternity to complete.

Yann is not only a photographer whom I admire; he is also my friend. I know him better than anyone, and I can testify to the charismatic force of his personality. This is clear from this work itself, which required the participation of an incredible number of people. Yann recruited and challenged them, and they responded to him.

The following pages are the most wonderful way he could have thanked them.

Hervé de La Martinière
Managing Director, La Martinière Groupe

CONTENTS

*Captions in the photographic sections were written by
Astrid Avundo and Frédéric Marchand*

Title page
**GORGES OF THE BRAS DE CAVERNE,
Island of Réunion, France**
Access to the interior of Réunion is made difficult by the numerous gorges of the Bras de Caverne River, which cuts its bed through the volcanic breaks of the Cirque de Salazie. Certain sites were not explored until quite recently, such as the Trou de Fer (Iron Hole), a ravine 820 feet (250 m) deep that was first explored in 1989. Thus preserved from human interference, the tropical forest on the volcanic relief of the island has maintained its primal condition, featuring giant thorns, ferns, and lichens; the forest at lower altitudes has been converted into agricultural or urban regions and has disappeared. More than thirty animal or vegetable species, including approximately twenty that were endemic to the island, have become extinct here in the past four centuries. Island systems have tremendous biological diversity, but they usually experience a higher rate of species extinction.

Previous spread
**BOAT ON THE NILE,
Egypt**
The world's second-longest river, the Nile travels through Sudan and Egypt for 4,140 miles (6,671 km). It serves as a means of transport for luxury cruise ships as well as modest boats holding grains. The Nile is the country's main source of water, supplying 90 percent of the water for consumption. At one time the Nile's annual floods only guaranteed available water for three to four months, but the building of the Aswan Dam in the 1960s regulated the river's rate of flow, providing Egypt with water throughout the year. The dam, however, has created major ecological problems: it deprives the river of the silt that fertilized the soil and offset marine erosion of the delta, which is today retreating at a rate between 100 and 650 feet (30 to 200 m) per year.

THE STATE OF THE WORLD
IN THE YEAR 2000

How will history evaluate the year 2000? Calendar landmarks, of course, do not always correspond to turning points in world history. Yet it is popular today to see the new century as the threshold to the era of globalization. Is there any merit to this view? Since the early 1980s, swift upheaval in the financial cycles has given rise to a capital market that is uniquely vigorous, and international trade is responding to the advancing triumph of free markets. The internationalization of production, a much older phenomenon, has also intensified. Large corporations, involved in gigantic mergers and restructuring, are expanding their overseas presence, and direct investment is enjoying an unprecedented boom in the triad of North America, Europe, and Japan.

This globalization has been energized by the appearance of "emerging markets" born from the economic resurgence of East Asia and, more recently, from the collapse of the Soviet bloc and the Chinese economy's conversion—in a forced march—to capitalism. Internationalization is also enhanced by the formation of great regional units, common markets such as the European Union or Mercosur in Latin America, or free trade zones such as NAFTA in North America. These economic trends are paired with an acceleration of the blending of cultures; of the speed of communication all over the world, including the exchange of information and images in real time; and of the volume of cross-national transactions.

Nevertheless, we cannot say for certain that our descendants will remember these phenomena as having marked a significant rupture in the long history of the world. Other processes are at work, notably developments in science and technology, not to mention possible geopolitical upheavals of great scope, which may well come to seem more decisive. Moreover, if the times we are living in seem to be marked by the transnational and supranational phenomena of globalism, local forces are also gaining strength and acquiring new political significance.

Our planet in the year 2000 has approximately 6 billion people, 20 percent of whom live in developed countries and 80 percent in the developing world. Asia alone accounts for 60 percent of the world population. This world is increasingly urban. According to the United Nations Population Fund (UNPF), 45 percent of the world population lives in cities (the figure is 75 percent for developed countries and only 22 percent in the less developed countries or LDC). Forty-one metropolises have more than 5 million inhabitants (half of them have more than 10 million); three-quarters are located in developing countries.

The population is still growing at a uniform rate, but the birthrate has begun to decline perceptibly in every continent. In twenty years the global average has dropped from 3.92 children per woman to 2.79 (5.31 in Africa, 2.65 in Asia and Latin America, and 1.45 in Europe). Today the world population is young: 30 percent is below fifteen years of age and only 6.8 percent is over sixty-five.

RIGHTS OF NATIONS, HUMAN RIGHTS, AND WOMEN'S RIGHTS

The 6 billion people of today are distributed within the territory of 193 sovereign states. One hundred years ago great empires—Ottoman, Russian, Austro-Hungarian, German, British, French, Dutch, Belgian—still covered most of the planet. The twentieth century will go down as the age of decolonization, if not the age of emancipation, as each nation aspires to self-government and self-determination. The disappearance of empires, however, has not put an end to hegemonic claims of power. Similarly, conflicts have not disappeared along with the Cold War, even if the end of the East-West confrontation has deeply changed the meaning of them. These conflicts continue to create rootless people. The number of refugees in the world has been estimated at about 50 million, the victims of forced displacement through wars, persecutions, discrimination, and other violent acts.

In the course of the last two decades, many dictatorships and authoritarian regimes have fallen in Latin America and the Soviet Bloc, Asia and Africa. Many countries still live under the yoke of tyranny, but the struggle for freedom and human rights has a promising future.

The world remains dominated by men, who overwhelmingly control the political and economic spheres. However, despite widespread discrimination against women throughout the world, some of the most blatant inequalities show signs of weakening, especially in the areas of education and health. Between 1970 and 1990 the literacy gap between female and male populations decreased by half; the average primary school enrollment of girls has reached 90 percent of the enrollment rate for boys, according to statistics of UNESCO (United Nations Education, Scientific, and Cultural Organization). In certain regions of the world, however, females are still barred from education.

In the space of twenty years, the life expectancy of women has risen 20 percent more quickly than that of men. However, the number of deaths in childbirth per 100,000 live births remains alarmingly high in Africa (878), southern Asia (562), Southeast Asia (443), and the Caribbean (408). The gap with developed countries is considerable: in northern Europe, Canada, and the United States the number is 11 per 100,000. Women's growing autonomy in the decision to have children, however, seems to be an irreversible gain. The

ability to limit births by contraceptive methods has made it possible to distinguish sexuality from procreation. Some countries, however, still use coercive methods to enforce birth control.

WEALTH AND POVERTY

The violent Asian crisis that erupted in the summer of 1997 must not cause us to overlook the economic readjustments at work for more than twenty years on a global scale. In 1997 the world gross domestic product (GDP), a measure of the wealth produced during the year, stabilized at $32,735 billion (after corrections to account for the differences in purchasing power between countries). Half of this wealth is produced by North America (especially the United States, with 25 percent), the European Union (Germany, France, United Kingdom, and Italy alone making up 13 percent), and East Asia (especially Japan, with 9 percent).

In the same year world exports totaled $5,400 billion. The industrialized countries claimed a share of two-thirds of this pie, a lower proportion than in 1970 (76.2 percent). The share of developing countries advanced globally between these two dates (to 33.5 percent from 23.8 percent). Asia went from 5.8 to 19.1 percent, but Africa fell from 4.4 to 2.3 percent and Latin America from 5.6 to 4.3 percent. Among developed countries, Japan won a greater share than before.

The hierarchy among industrialized nations has changed markedly over the past twenty years. According to the Organization for Economic Cooperation and Development (OECD), in 1977 Japan's GDP per inhabitant was 62.8 percent of the United States figure; by 1997 it had risen to 81.2 percent of the United States figure. The proportion between the European Union and the United States has also grown closer, but only by five percentage points.

In the area of technological progress, the twentieth century has seen a permanent revolution. The United States, the countries of western Europe, and Japan share the bulk of this innovation: the 1996 statistics of UNESCO state that these nations are the originators of 55.6, 15.3, and 21 percent, respectively, of the patents in the United States. These same countries provide 80 percent of research and development efforts, while China, Taiwan, Singapore, and South Korea count for 10 percent.

In 1960 the richest one-fifth of the world's population had a revenue thirty times higher than the poorest one-fifth; in 1995, according to a comparable study, the richest group's revenue was 82 times higher. The 1998 annual report of the United Nations Development Programme (UNDP) estimates that 225 of the largest fortunes in the world represent a total of more than $1,000 billion. On the average, in 1998 the annual GDP per inhabitant of the fifteen wealthiest nations of the world exceeded $20,000, whereas the figure for the fifteen poorest countries was below $1,000. Between Luxembourg (more than $30,000) and Mozambique ($500), the gap was more than sixty to one. On top of this is the question of foreign debt: for developing countries as a whole, it represented more than $2,000 billion in 1997. However, the inequalities are not only between wealthy nations, the majority of which are located in the Northern Hemisphere, and poor countries, typically in the Southern Hemisphere. Inequality within each individual nation is a crucial concern as well.

FUNDAMENTAL NEEDS AND HUMAN DEVELOPMENT

The degree to which certain basic needs are satisfied, needs such as nutrition, access to drinking water, health, education, and shelter, is highly indicative of the condition of populations and of societies and of their "human development," a term made popular by the UNDP.

Three centuries ago the average age of death was approximately the same everywhere in the world. People died at about the age of thirty, and only two out of three children lived to the age of five. Today the life expectancy on earth has more than doubled (65.6 years on a global average), but the gaps remain immense: over the age of 75 in the United States, Canada, and western Europe, versus an age of 53.8 in Africa. However, in twenty-six years, the life expectancy in developing countries rose from 46 to 62—almost 70 in East Asia and Latin America but only 50 in sub-Saharan Africa).

Globally, infant mortality, measured as the rate of death of children less than one year old per thousand live-born children, continues to decrease. The world average in twenty years went from 87 to 57 per 1,000. In developing countries the average declined by more than half in forty years, but considerable inequalities persist. The situation in many countries remains acute: the infant mortality rate is 86 per 1,000 in Africa, approximately eight times more than the prevailing level in North America and western Europe.

To a great extent, the persistence of a high infant mortality rate (9 million children under one year of age still die each year in the poorer countries) is due to poor hygienic conditions, particularly the absence of basic sanitation and the lack of drinking water. About 30 percent of the population in developing countries do not have drinking water; indeed, in developing countries four out of five illnesses are linked to water. In industrialized nations the situation is totally different: two out of five mortalities result from cardiovascular disease and cancer, both of which are typical of societies of plenty.

Approximately 800 million people still suffer from hunger, notably in Africa and Asia. The most developed nations, for their part, consume more than 50 percent of primary energy although they make up only 20 percent of world population.

Turning to the field of education, we can point to undeniable progress, although global averages mask strong disparities. Between 1970 and 1995, adult literacy levels in developing countries advanced from 48 to 70 percent although the figure remains at 51 percent in southern Asia. The number of university students continues to grow. In the 1990s, according to UNESCO, the most developed countries (United States, Canada, Japan, and the countries of western Europe) accounted for about 45 percent of those enrolled in universities (24 percent for the United States and Canada alone).

THE FUTURE EARTH

In the 1980s environmental problems, formerly only of local concern, took on global proportions and triggered debates, demonstrations, conferences, and international negotiations. The stakes are enormous: to preserve the common heritage of the human race.

For millennia human beings transformed the natural world, without upsetting the earth's fundamental balances. It was only in the twentieth century—and particularly within the last fifty years—that the first dangerous ruptures in these equilibriums occurred. They were born of two vertiginous accelerations in the earth's development: population growth and technological change. These accelerations, in turn, led to greater inequality among people, pollution of many kinds, a squandering of resources, and a reduction in the number of species. In addition, with the knowledge gained in the fields of genetics and biotechnology, humans can henceforth claim—not without some danger—to have "reinvented nature" and to have disturbed a portion of the earth's ecosystems.

Faced with this situation, we cannot simply seek refuge in the contemplation of places where "natural" nature seems to have been preserved. The landscapes of today were fashioned over the course of time by different civilizations. An examination of how human societies have appropriated their environments is a prerequisite for taking stock of the basic challenges we face in the next century: the population explosion, feeding the planet, the distribution of wealth, climatic dangers, and the future of urban civilization.

It is this conviction that inspires the authors of the chapters in this book. Renowned specialists in their fields—geography, history of science, ecology, sociology, demography, economy, and philosophy—they have put their expertise to use in interpreting the future in the light of their respective knowledge and the lessons of history. In this way they contribute toward a picture of the state of the world in the year 2000. This diverse study complements the magnificent photographs by Yann Arthus-Bertrand, who presents through the distance of his aerial lens a different kind of "inventory" of the planet; these photographs offer views of a nature apparently still intact, interspersed with sights of construction and human activity. An inspiring way to mark a date.

Serge Cordellier
Editorial Director of the annual *L'état du monde*
(Éditions La Découverte)

p. 17
HIMBA COUPLE,
Kaokoland region, Namibia
The region of Kaokoland in northern Namibia is home to 3,000 to 5,000 Himba, nomadic herders of cows and goats who live along the Cunene River. This people, which has maintained its traditions and lives outside the modern world, suffered twin disasters in the 1980s: a long drought that killed three-fourths of the livestock and the war between the South African Army and SWAPO (South West Africa People's Organization). Today the Himba face a threat that is equally important: the planned construction of a hydroelectric dam on the Epupa Falls. This project, which would provide power for a water desalination plant in a country that imports nearly 50 percent of its electricity and is greatly deprived of water resources, would also result in the flooding of hundreds of square miles of pastureland, forcing the Himba herders to migrate to new lands.

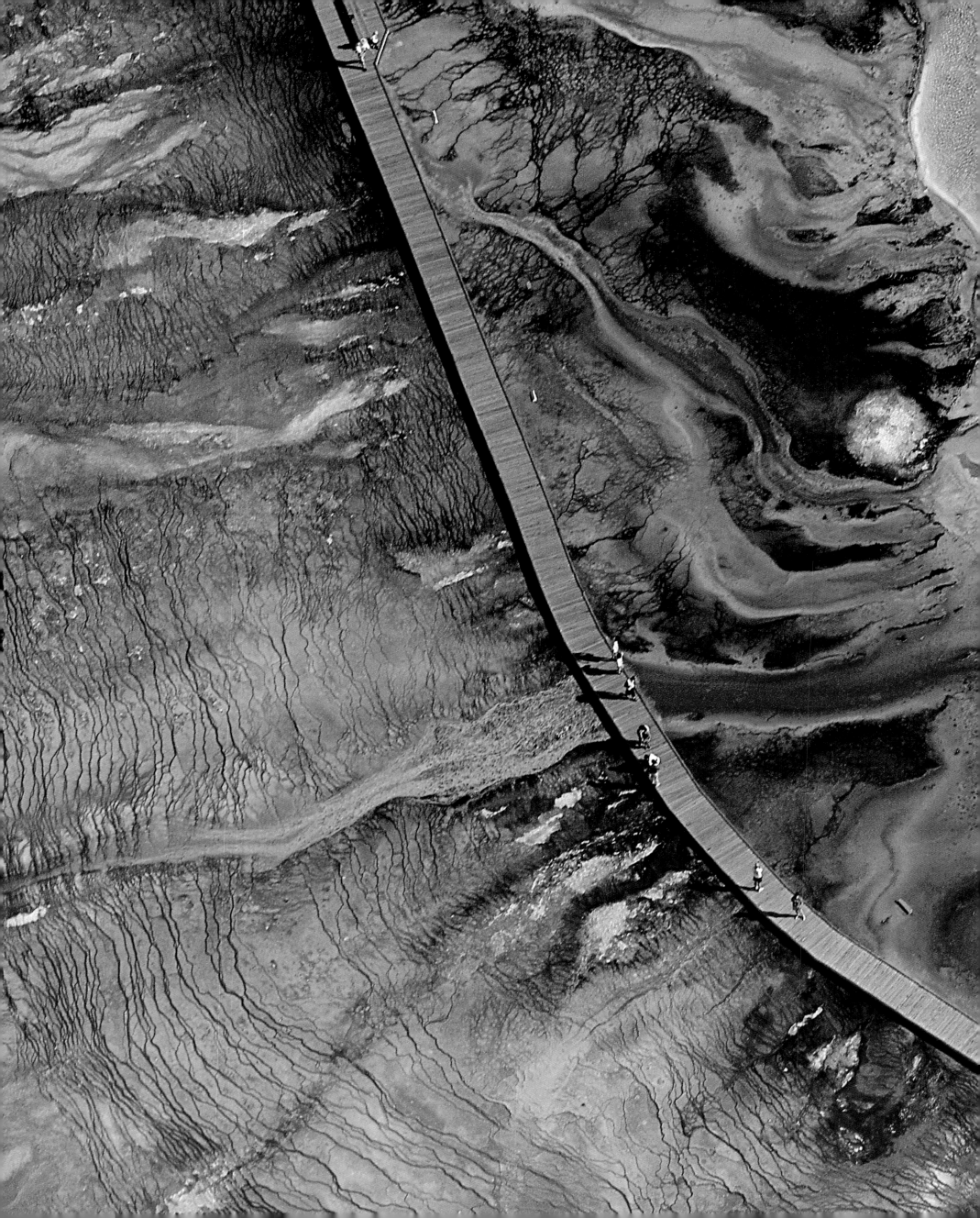

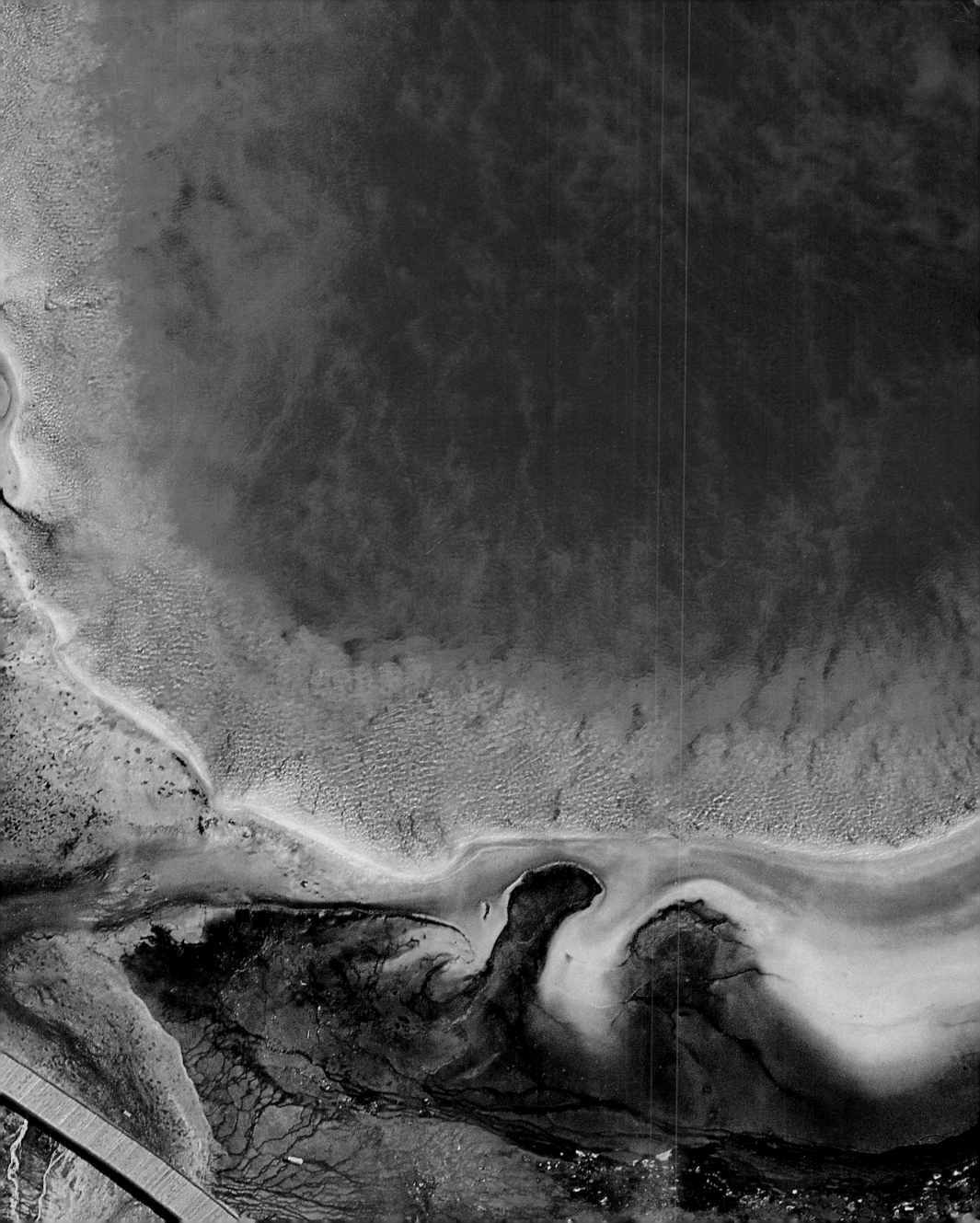

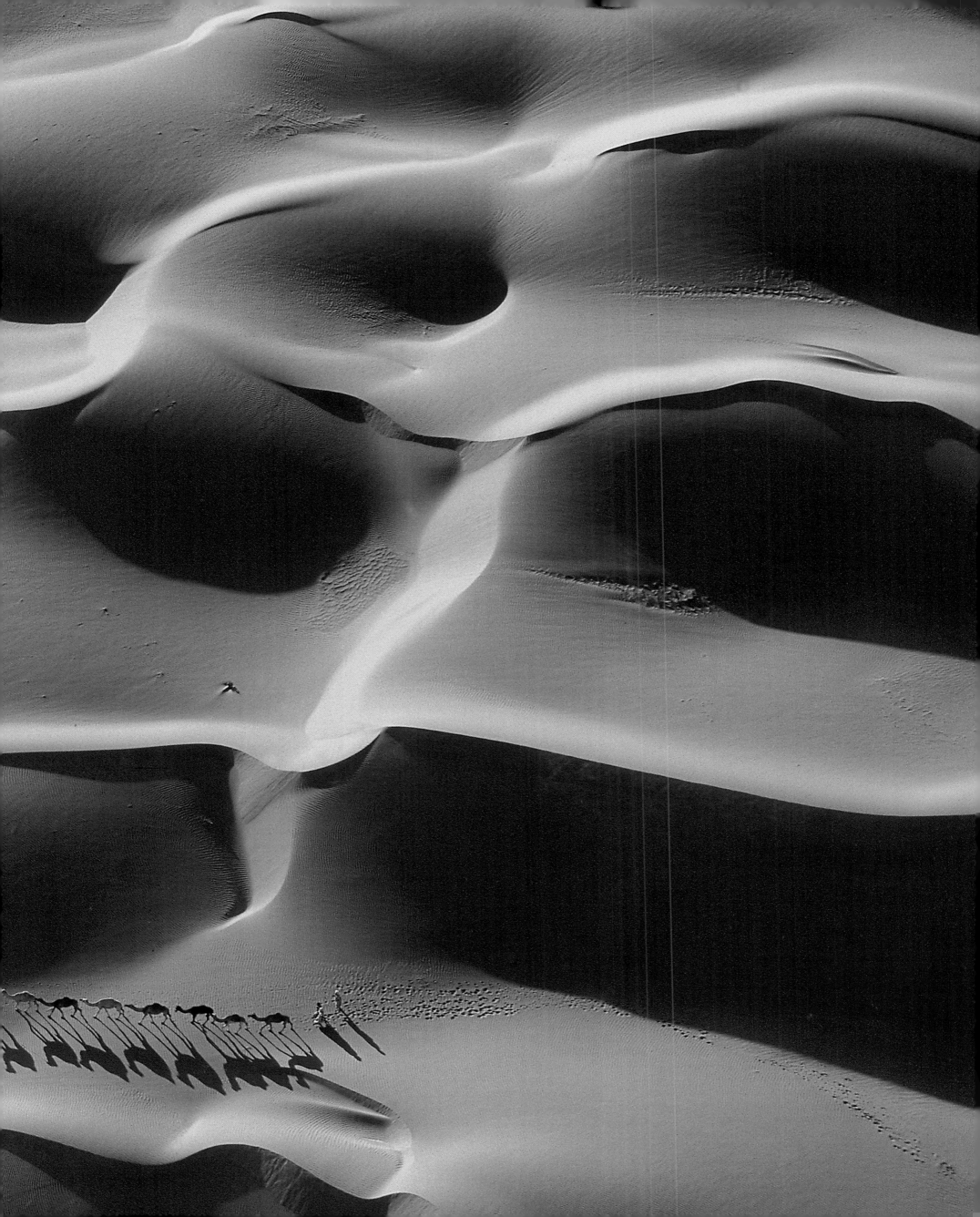

FROM THE PALEOLITHIC AGE TO GLOBALIZATION

The human being is a product of nature. Our species shares 98 percent of its genetic material with our closest species relative, the chimpanzee—a fact that seems even more incredible when we realize that human beings are only 99.8 percent similar to each other. We are members of the animal kingdom, indissolubly bound to the environment, despite our perceived superiority to other species. Nonetheless, the claim to being "outside" nature is perhaps justified by the human capacity to transform its environment.

This ability has long been considered a gift peculiar to the species, whether this claim is true or not, giving humankind carte blanche to use nature without restraint and without regard for consequences. Because of our exercise of this freedom ever since the Paleolithic era, humankind at the dawn of a new millennium is confronted with unforeseen, if not unforeseeable, obstacles. In a growing number of instances, this license has turned into abuse—what was a boon has become a threat to the species.

The human race has managed to extricate itself from nature and manipulate it to such an extent that the environment, the very foundation of life, is now severely imperiled—and thus the future of humanity is in danger as well. Today, faced with the terrible consequences of our abuses, we realize that we are not free to do what we like. We are an integral part of nature and are dependent upon it.

THE HUMAN DISTINCTION

At one time we believed that humans alone had the ability to think and to have self-consciousness. However, it has recently been discovered that chimpanzees also have the capacity for self-consciousness, forcing us to redefine our notion of what is distinctively human. For years to come science will continue to give us second thoughts about domains we had considered purely our own. Who would have believed only a few years ago that it would be demonstrated that certain species of ants, insects living in organized societies with

p. 48
EROSION ON THE SLOPES OF A VOLCANO NEAR ANKISABE,
near Antananarivo, Madagascar
The origins of the Malagasy people are little known; the first residents apparently settled on the island a mere 2,000 years ago, arriving from Africa and Indonesia in successive waves of migration. For centuries the island has practiced traditional farming by slash-and-burn cultivation, known as *tavy*, which has been particularly devastating for the natural environment because of overexploitation in recent decades. Indeed, due to major demographic growth (the island's population has almost tripled in less than 30 years) and the planting of new crops such as corn since the 1930s, which require broader fields, Madagascar is undergoing rapid deforestation. Agricultural expansion has caused the disappearance of more than 80 percent of the primary forest that once covered 90 percent of the island at the turn of the century, and every year nearly 600 square miles (1,500 km²) of forest are destroyed. Deprived of vegetal cover, the humus and loose earth are stripped away by the rains, uncovering a layer of clay that is not fertile. Faced with the disappearance of arable land, the Malagasy peasants also exploit steep, hilly regions like the sheer sides of mountains, topography in which the risk of erosion is even greater.

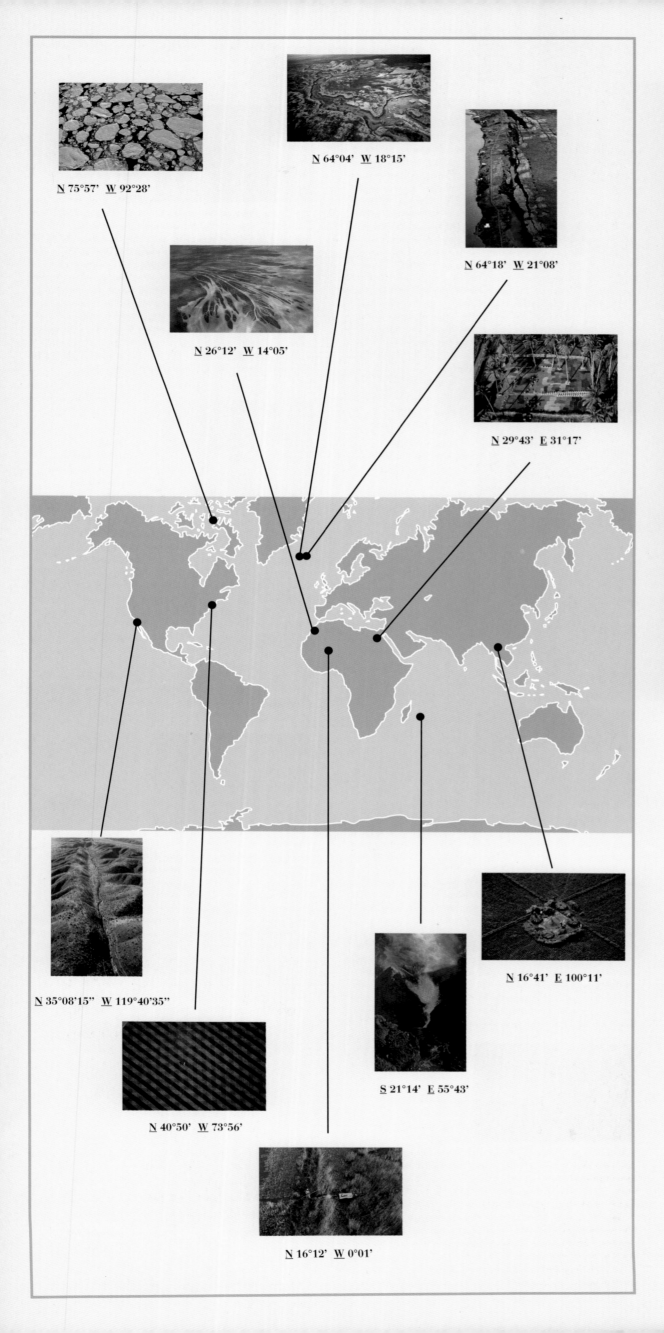

N 75°57’ <u>W</u> 92°28’

N 64°04’ <u>W</u> 18°15’

<u>N</u> 26°12’ <u>W</u> 14°05’

<u>N</u> 64°18’ <u>W</u> 21°08’

<u>N</u> 29°43’ <u>E</u> 31°17’

N 35°08’15” <u>W</u> 119°40’35”

<u>N</u> 40°50’ <u>W</u> 73°56’

<u>S</u> 21°14’ <u>E</u> 55°43’

<u>N</u> 16°41’ <u>E</u> 100°11’

<u>N</u> 16°12’ <u>W</u> 0°01’

INDIVIDUAL
CUMENE

mene—the area of the earth inhabited by
man beings, however tenuous their pres-
braces the entire planet. The ecumene
ety of environments and terrains; some
tial to others, as shown by either a den-
r a "void." Only recently have we become
significant facts. First, the ecumene was
independent of humanity; human inhab-
cological balances, and this modification
to make places unlivable. The second

important fact is that this ecumene only h

give to it, by our own intellectual constructi

The earth exists independently of us and

out us, but our existence depends on f

spaces that are hospitable to human hab

Today the equilibriums of our planet

sciousness of this threat has only recentl

an awareness that can take the form of no

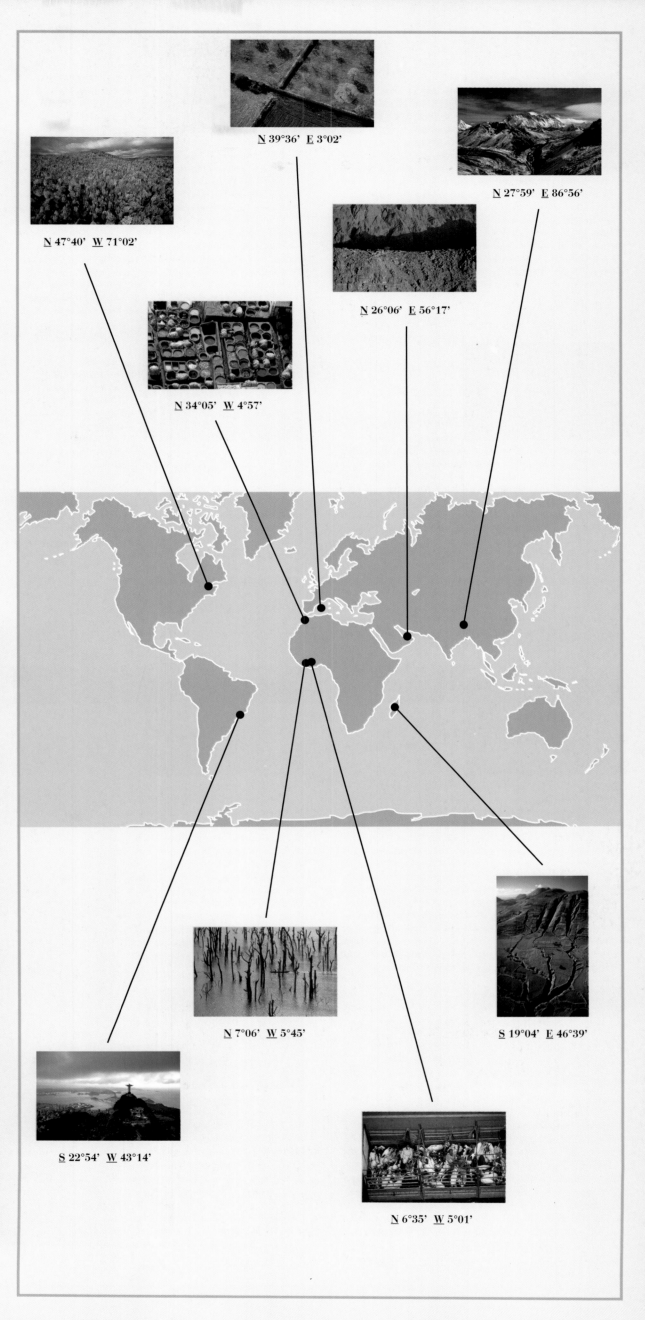

N 39°36' E 3°02'

N 27°59' E 86°56'

N 47°40' W 71°02'

N 26°06' E 56°17'

N 34°05' W 4°57'

S 19°04' E 46°39'

N 7°06' W 5°45'

S 22°54' W 43°14'

N 6°35' W 5°01'

with a growing sophistication in the ability to satisfy the ever-new needs of a carefree and increasingly comfortable society, while the widening network of the media has spread models of wealth across the globe. Yet the full weight of demographic growth falls most heavily on the most destitute. What would be the consequences for the environment, the world we inhabit, if the hundred poorest countries of the planet were to attain the same standard of living as the ten richest?

For the moment, only a small segment of society has arrived, undoubtedly with difficulty, at the conclusion that beliefs should remain private and, consequently, that the management of societies as well as of the environment should come under the control of the public sphere. Of course, individual and collective beliefs and general symbolic systems still play an important part in this management. New rights need to be recognized that will apply not only to one social group inhabiting one domain but to the entire human population throughout the world. The whole of the earth is progressively becoming the zone of reference for individuals in diverse societies.

Pierre Gentelle

---

p. 57
ERUPTIVE CONE OF PITON DE LA FOURNAISE,
island of Réunion, France
The Piton de la Fournaise ("Peak of the Furnace"), 8,600 feet (2,631 m) high, in southeastern Réunion, is the most active volcano on the planet after Kilauea in Hawaii. Active for the past 400,000 years, it erupts on an average of every 14 months; however, in the great majority of cases, the magma projections do not exceed the three zones of depressions, or *caldeiras*, that immediately surround it. Occasionally, as in 1977 and 1986, more violent eruptions occur in which destructive streams of lava invade the wooded slopes and the residential areas of the island. Today, 140 of the earth's 500 active volcanoes situated above sea level are permanently monitored by scientists. A volcanic observatory was built near the Piton de la Fournaise in 1979, making it one of the most closely watched volcanoes in the world.

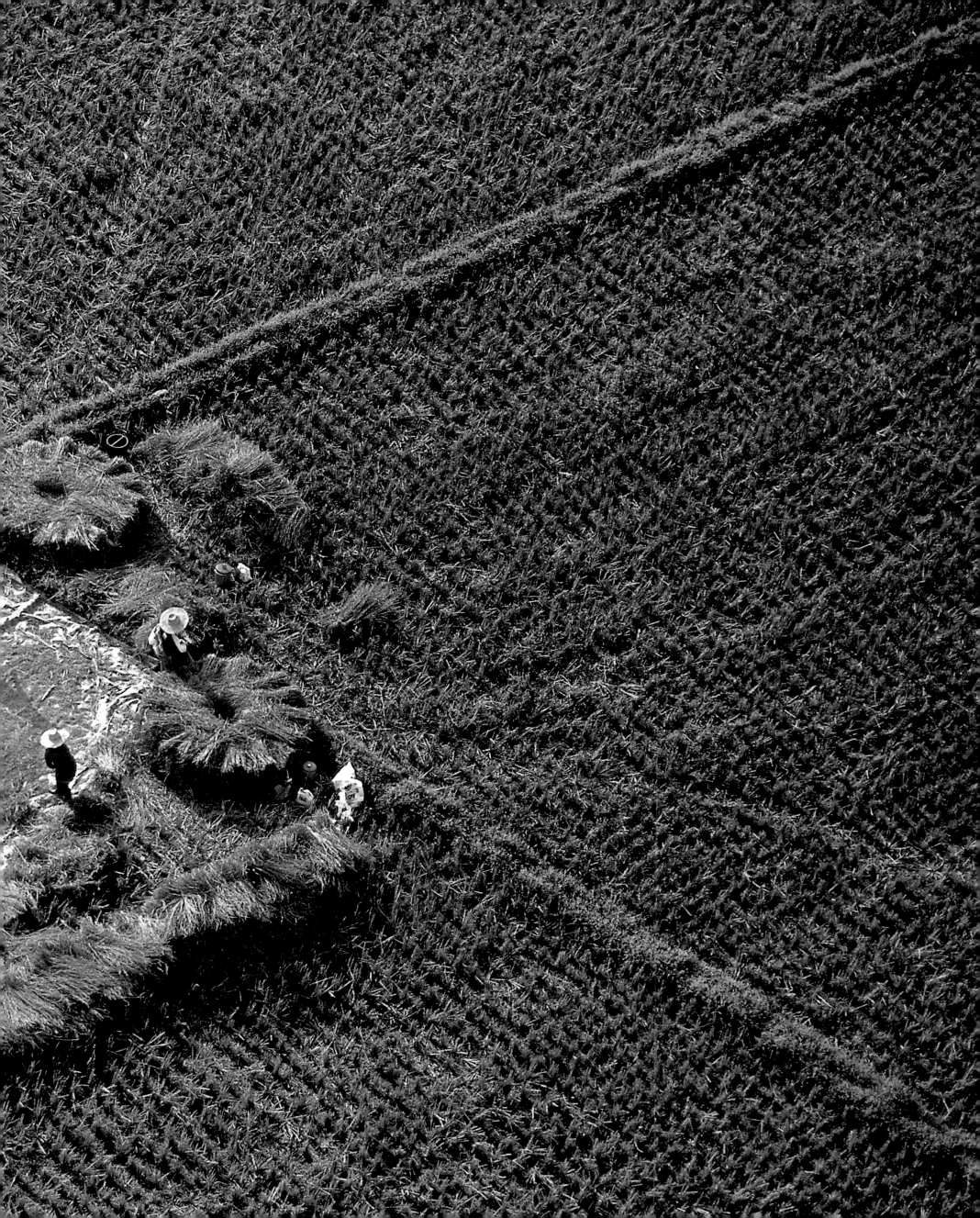

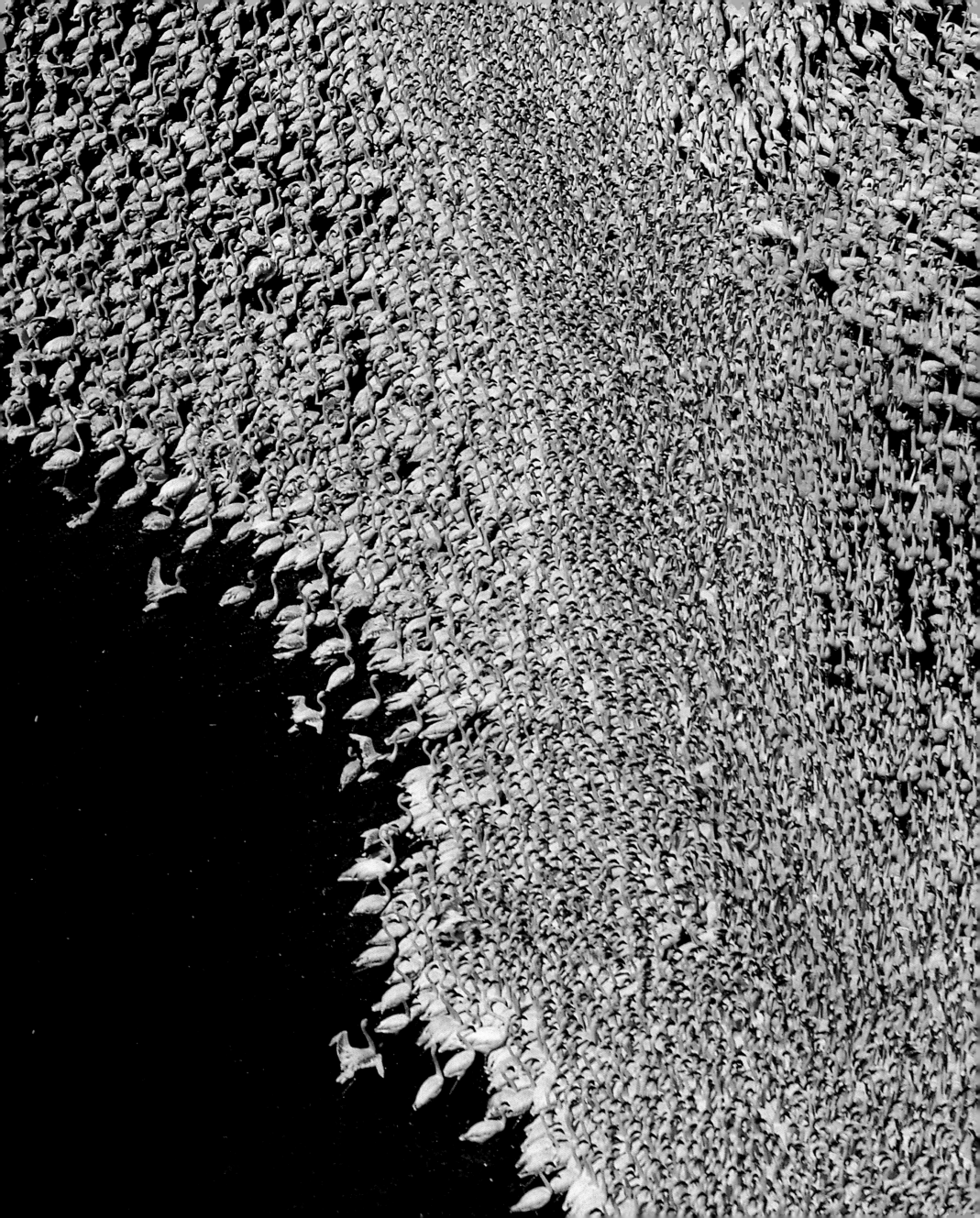

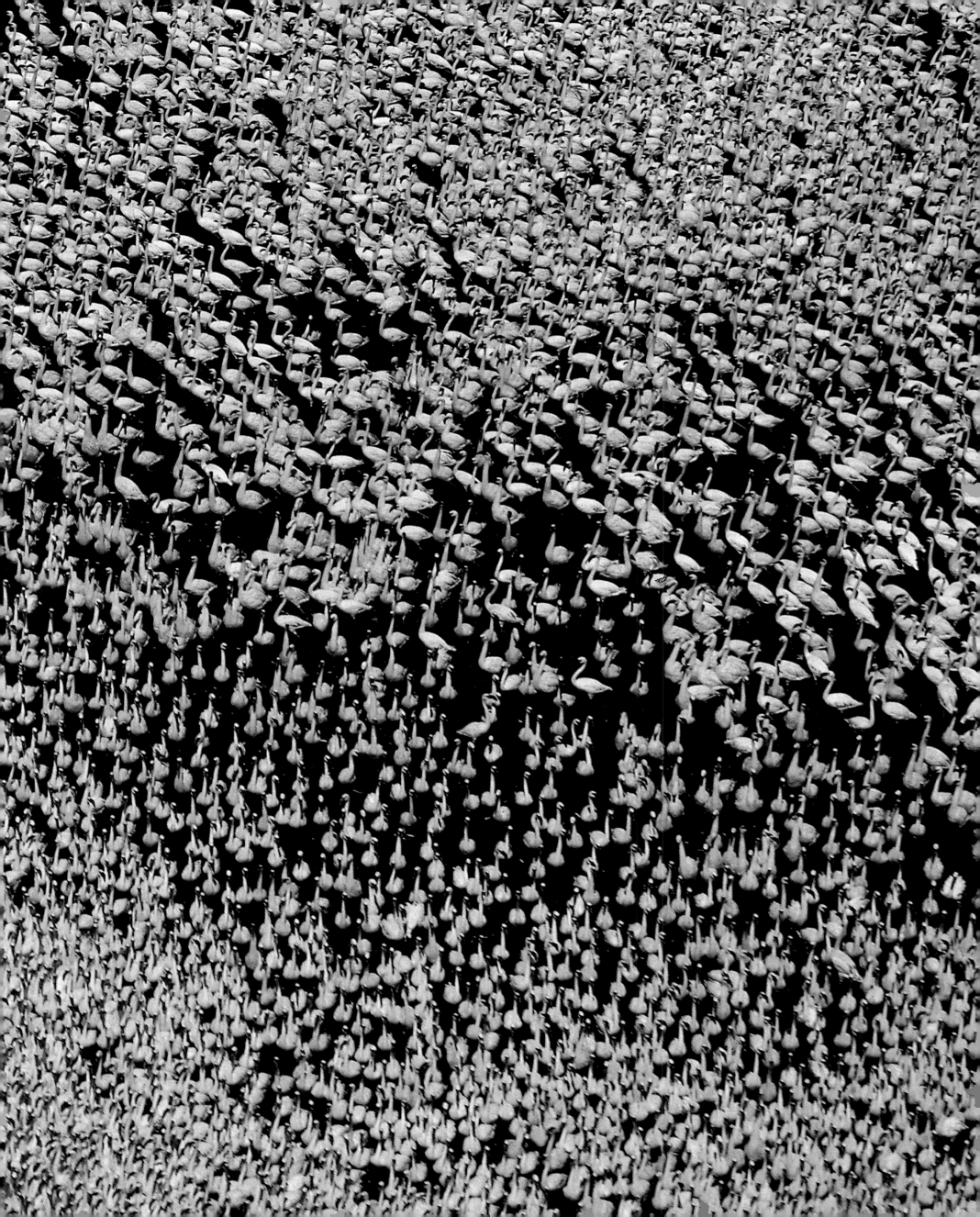

NATURE AND CULTURE

During the past one hundred thousand years the human species, *Homo sapiens sapiens*, produced a nourishing world within a cloud of beliefs intended to give meaning to the incomprehensible. In the development of humanity, the great landmark that followed the recognition of the self was the appearance of cults, which paid homage to nature, in its entirety or in some of its parts (sun, sky, rain), or to the human being itself, beginning with the dead. Rules governing how one lived soon developed, followed by laws and, much later, a system of rights and the constitutional state. This occurred in both hemispheres, north and south, and in every inhabited continent. Each highly structured civilization built a mythology attempting to explain the place of the human being in nature. Thus, the great religions and cosmogonies appeared: Hinduism and Buddhism, Confucianism and Shinto, Judaism, Islam, and Christianity. Present-day civilizations, the products of very powerful transformations, still navigate among these legacies.

THE STRUCTURE OF SOCIETY IN INDIA AND SOUTHEAST ASIA

The ancient beliefs of the peoples of Southeast Asia stated that natural space is never virgin: the removal of resources from nature first necessitated the placation of the gods preexisting in the place to be cultivated; only then could humans use nature for their own purposes. Under threat of catastrophes such as fires, invasions, or epidemics, people were required to constantly renew alliances with the gods or spirits. It was essential to mollify the displeased, and displaced, spirits and then to give them new lodging. The spirits had to understand that the good plots cleared by burning were not theirs and that they had to be content with the land considered least fruitful by humans. On that basis a functioning alliance was created in which the spirits were participants in a new order created by the human species.

The value system that structures Hindu civilization emphasizes the importance of the whole that constitutes soci-

p. 88
WASHING LAUNDRY IN A CREEK,
Adjamé district in Abidjan, Côte d'Ivoire
In the neighborhood of Adjamé in northern Abidjan, hundreds of professional launderers, the *fanicos*, do their wash every day in the creek located at the entrance of the forest of Le Banco (designated a national park in 1953). They use rocks and tires filled with sand to rub and wring the laundry, washing by hand thousands of articles of clothing. Formerly a fishing village, Adjamé is a working-class district without running water or electricity, absorbed gradually by the metropolis of Abidjan. This city of 3.5 million, one of the fastest-growing in West Africa (it multiplied 30 times in 40 years), has seen a proliferation of dozens of small trades in the informal sector, such as these *fanicos*.

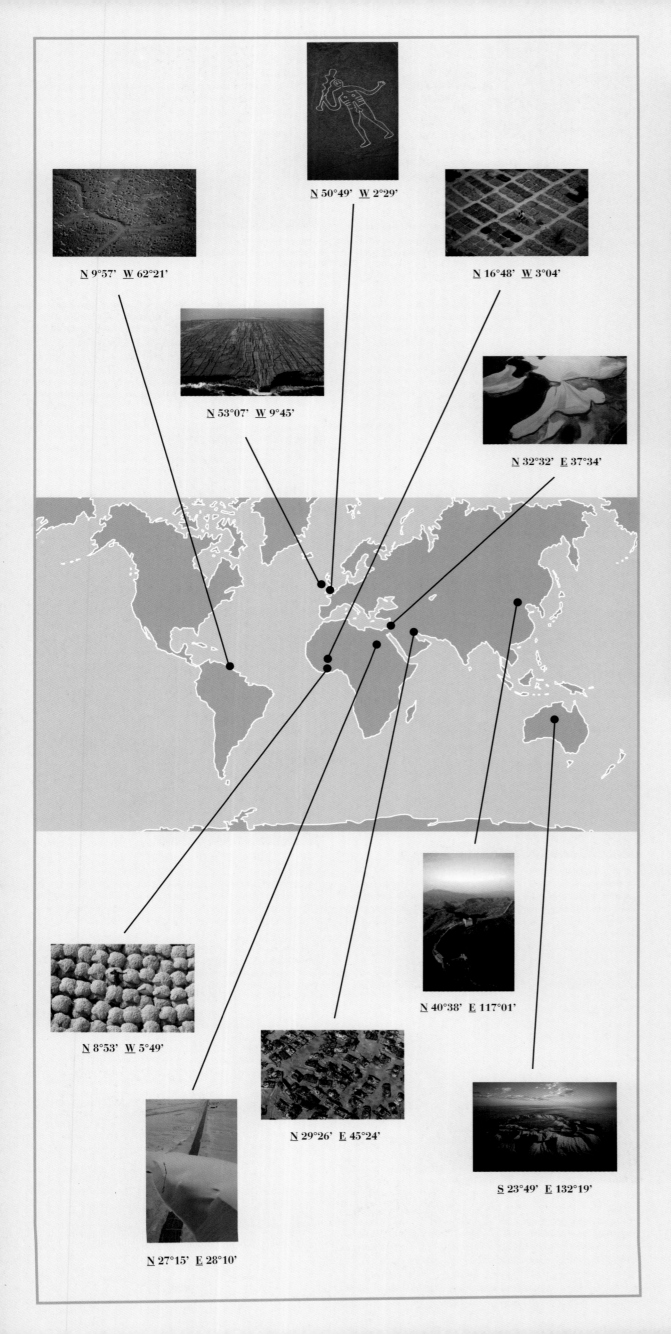

N 50°49' W 2°29'

N 9°57' W 62°21'

N 16°48' W 3°04'

N 53°07' W 9°45'

N 32°32' E 37°34'

N 40°38' E 117°01'

N 8°53' W 5°49'

N 29°26' E 45°24'

S 23°49' E 132°19'

N 27°15' E 28°10'

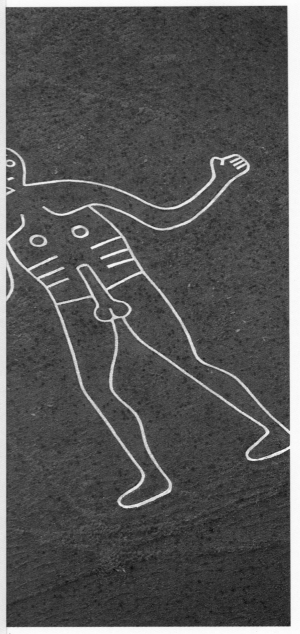

AND COSMOS
L ASIA

ntal belief of the Chinese world, along
phere of influence that included Korea,
, mandated that all human action obey
os, a law based on respect for proportions
ovement. For a happy life, people must
ns that prevail among the "objects of the
the human species. The neo-Confucians
ry called this "correct thinking." Philoso-
hinkers needed to interpret what actions
o cosmic law.

to century Chinese civilization thus built
ication of human actions, placed in the

preexisting categories of the cosmos. The

shan-shui, is not actually the basis for

human activities; it is only the expression,

of the cosmic order. The mountain, *shan*, i

yang, and flowing water (river, waterfall),

yin, of this energy. The relation between

is the explanation of all motion in the co

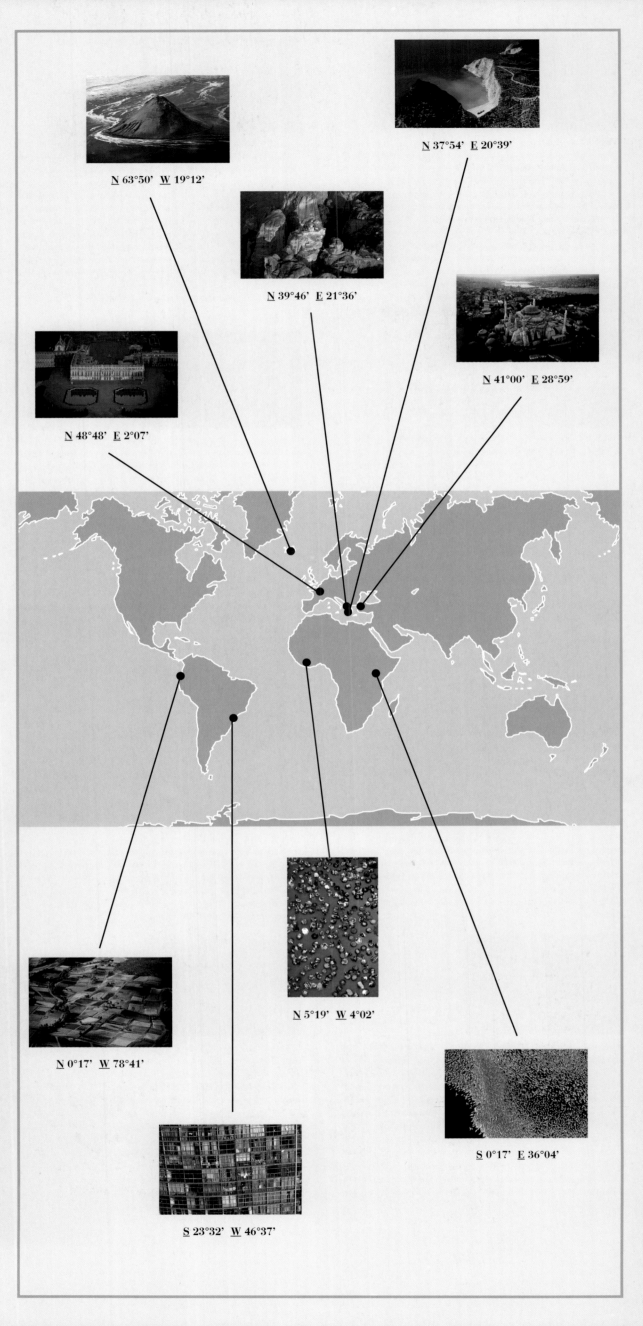

N 63°50' W 19°12'

N 37°54' E 20°39'

N 39°46' E 21°36'

N 41°00' E 28°59'

N 48°48' E 2°07'

N 5°19' W 4°02'

N 0°17' W 78°41'

S 0°17' E 36°04'

S 23°32' W 46°37'

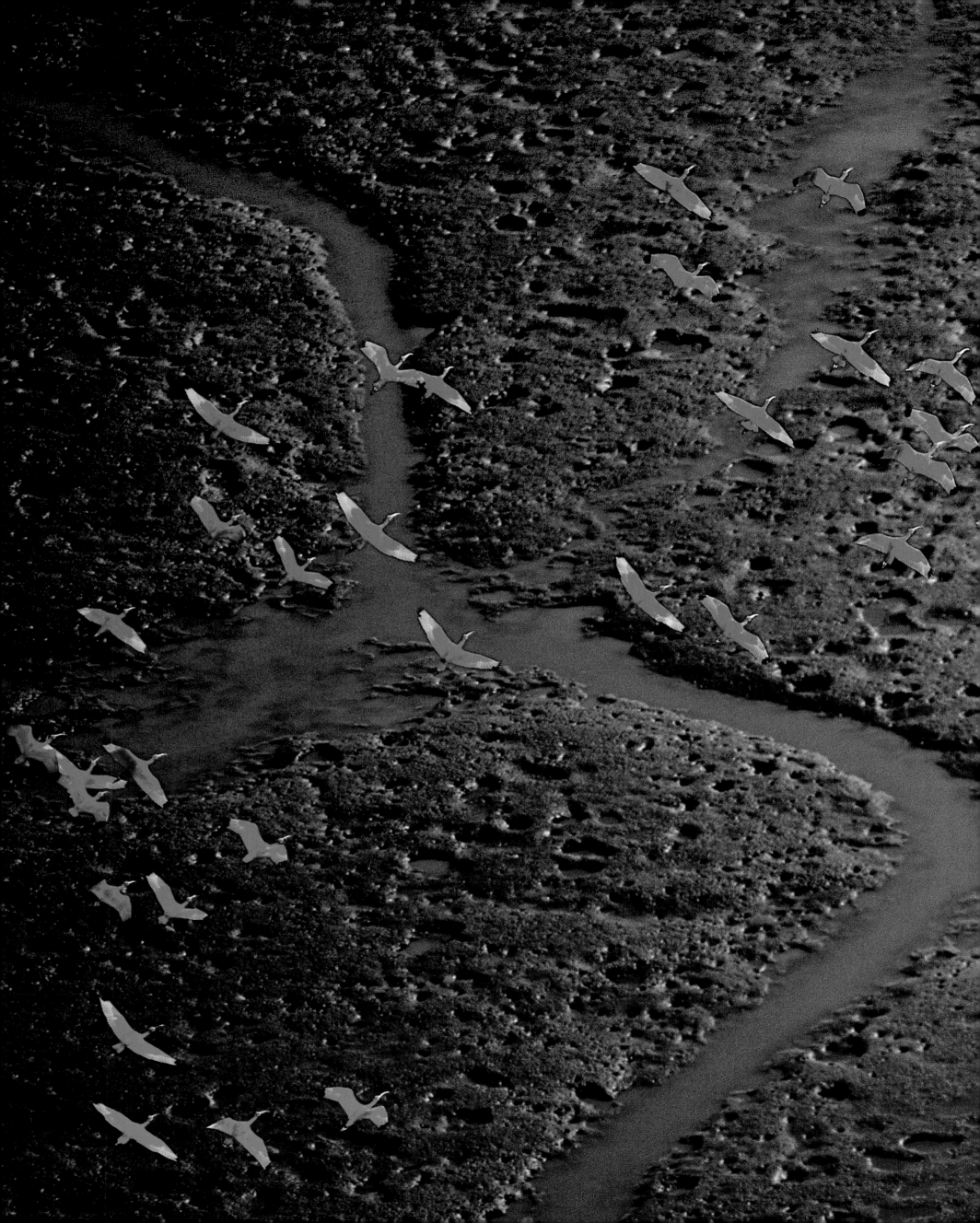

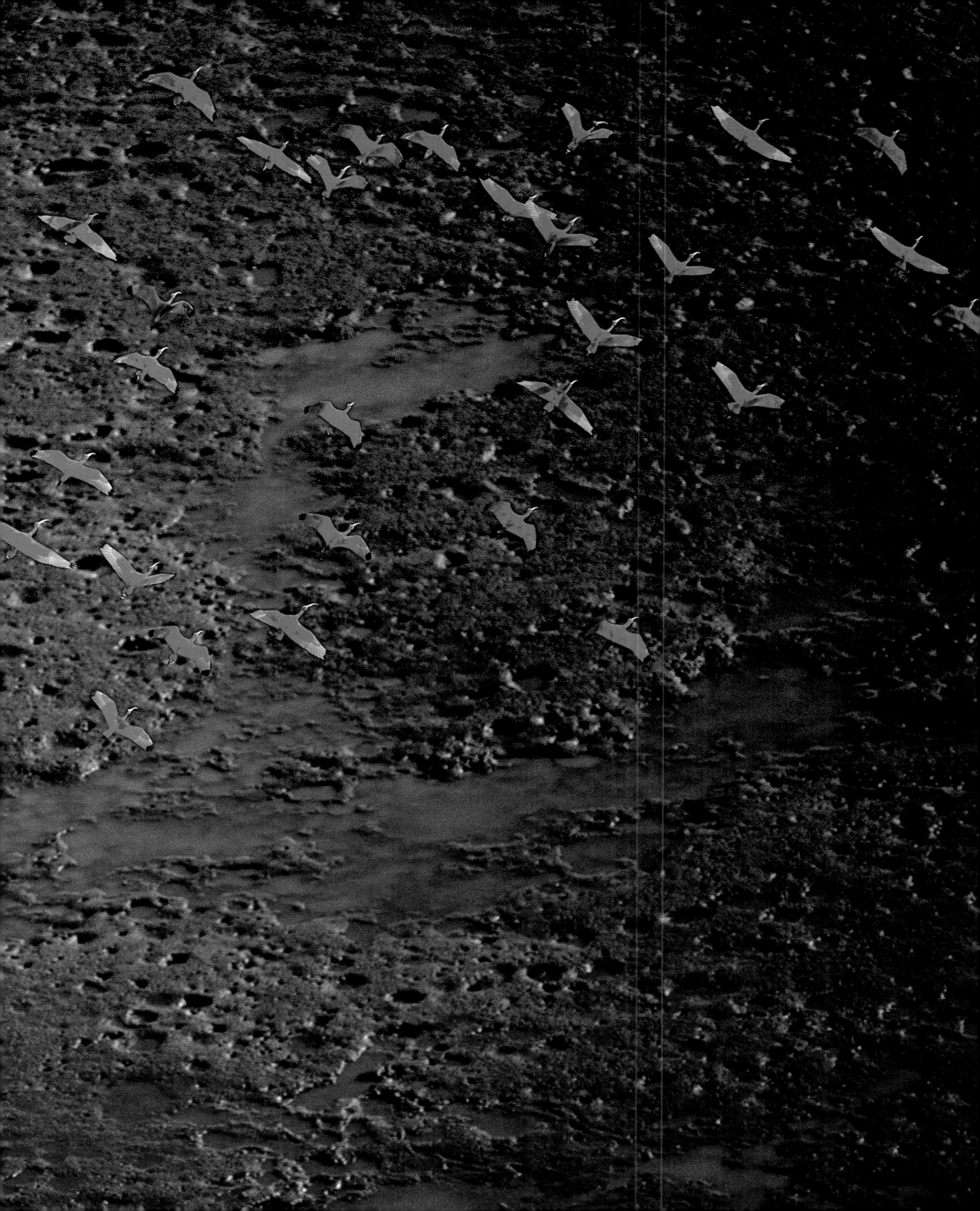

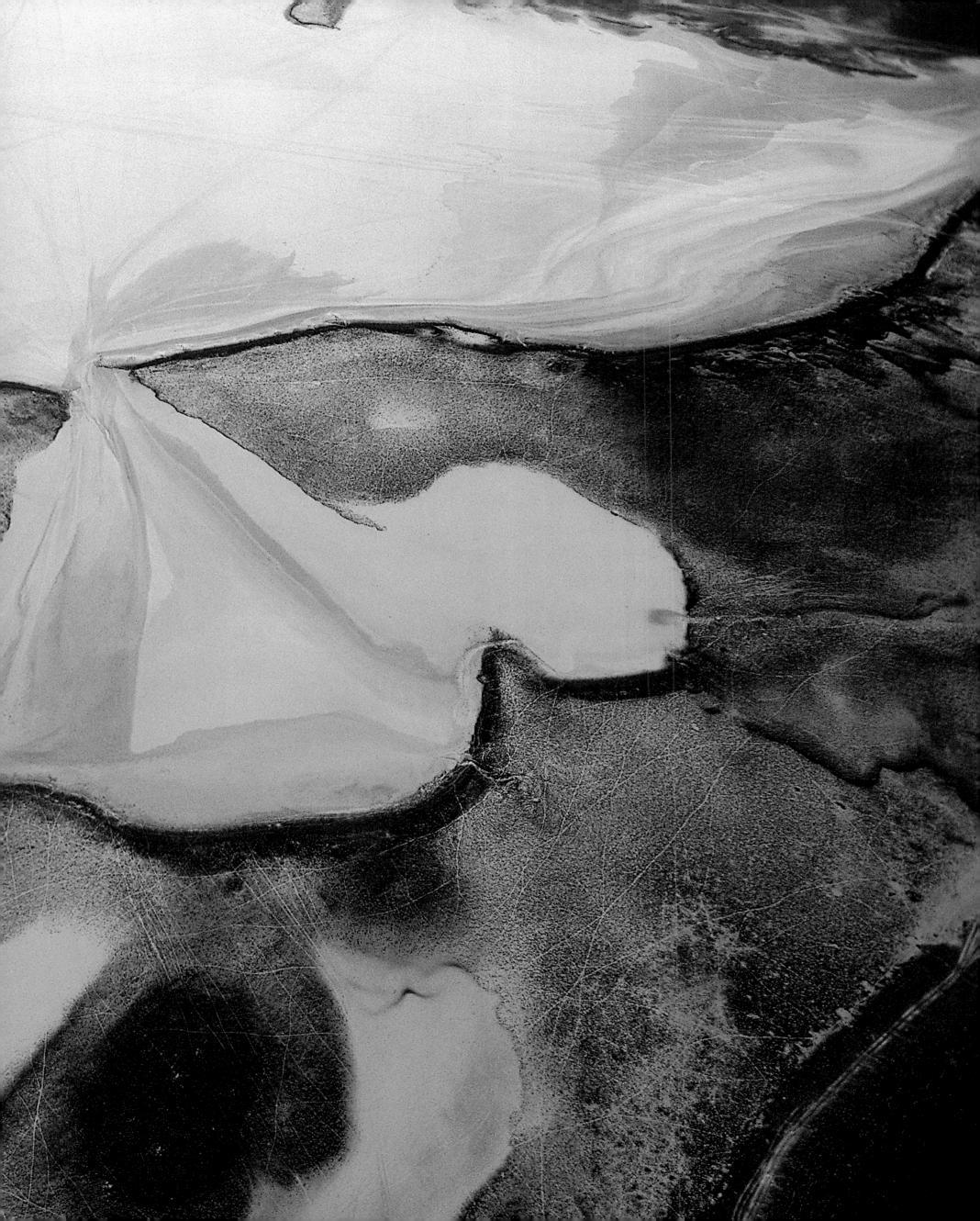

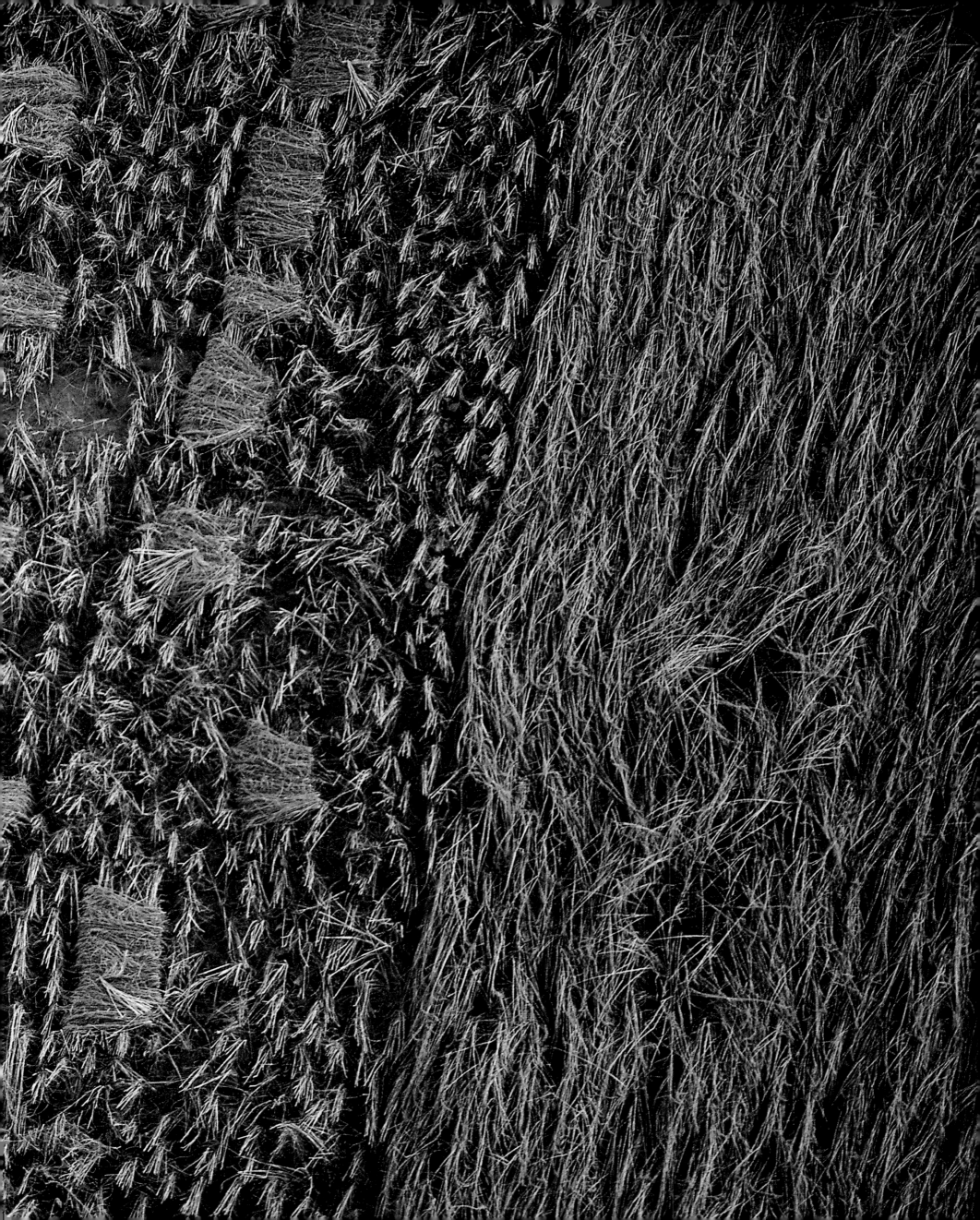

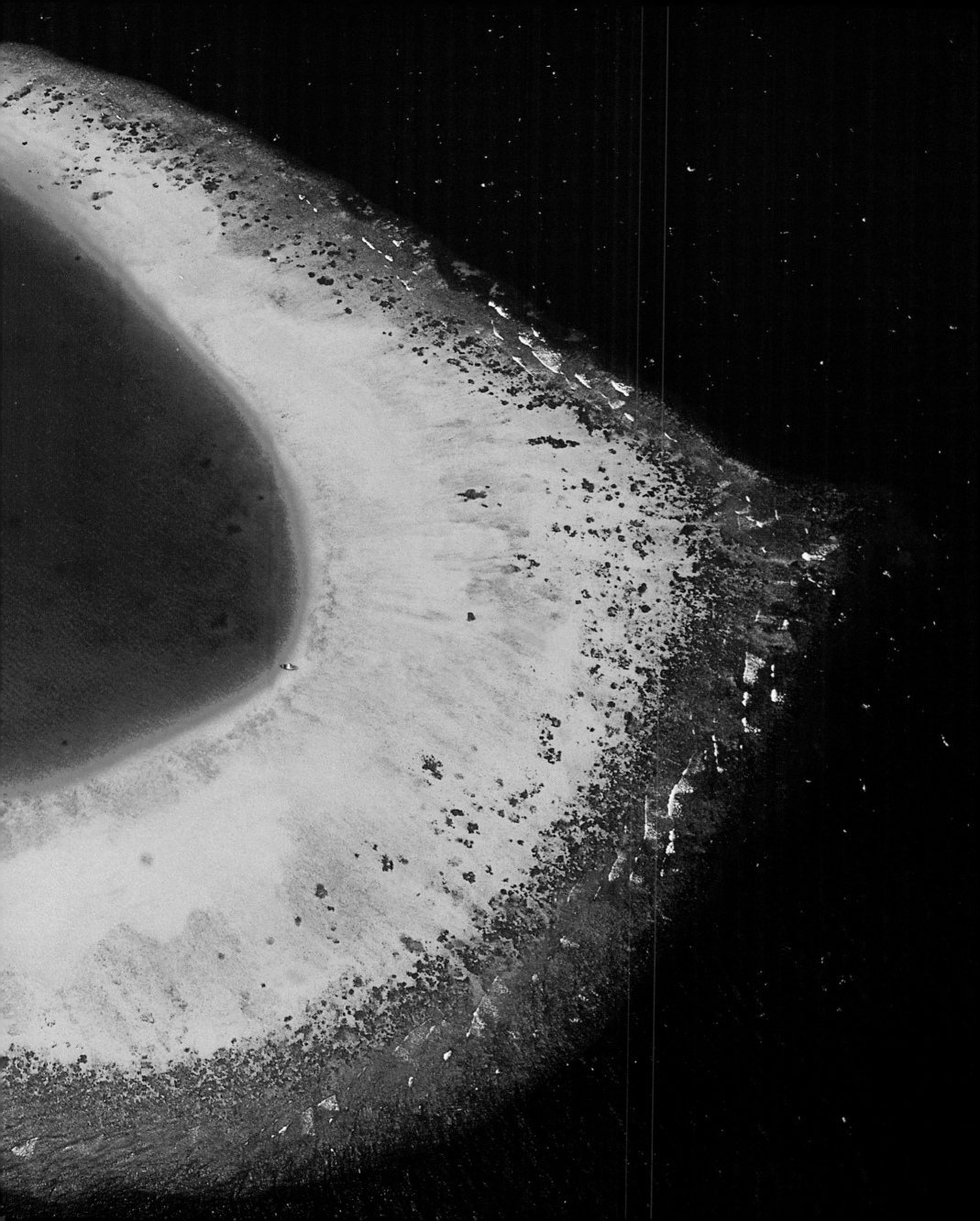

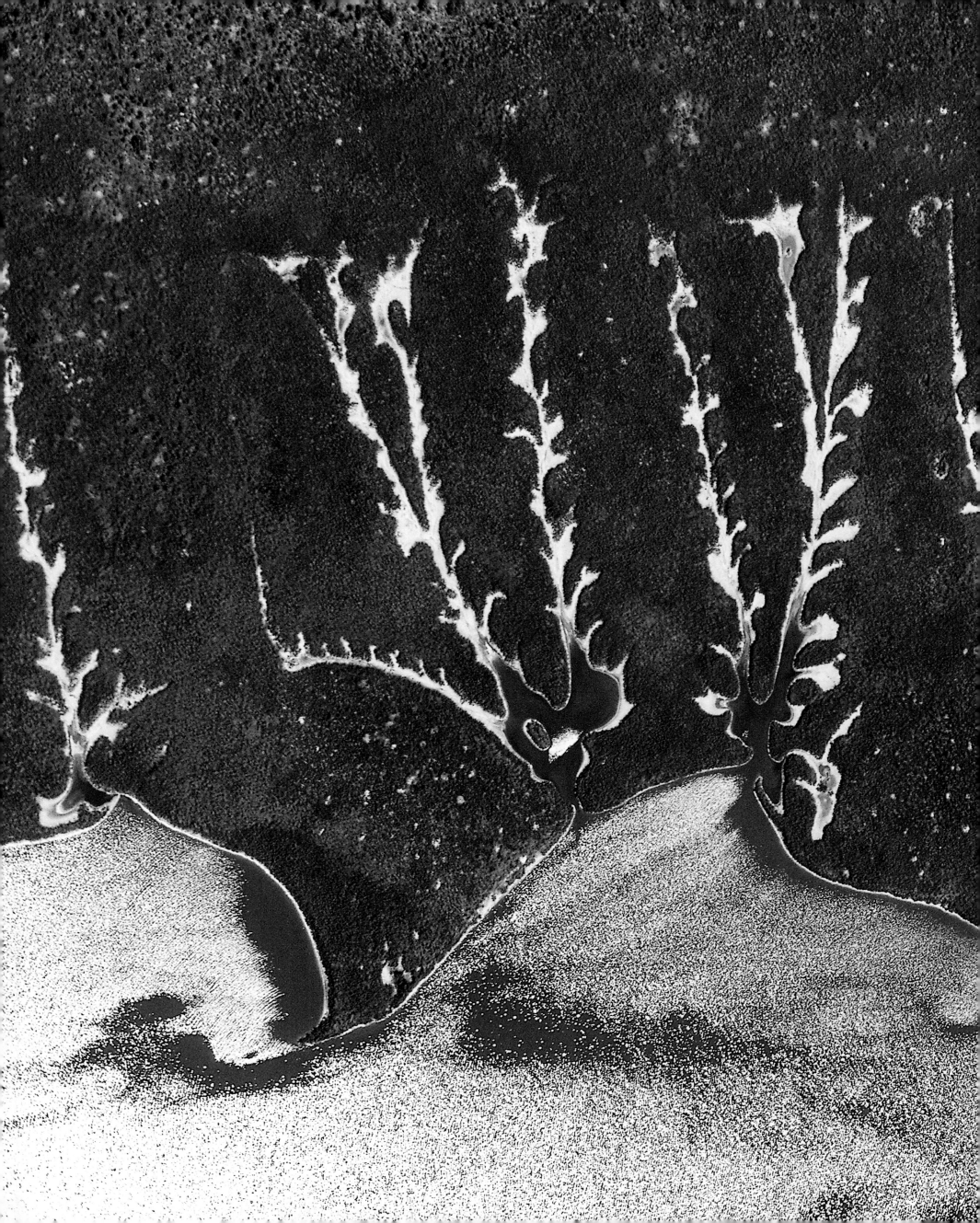

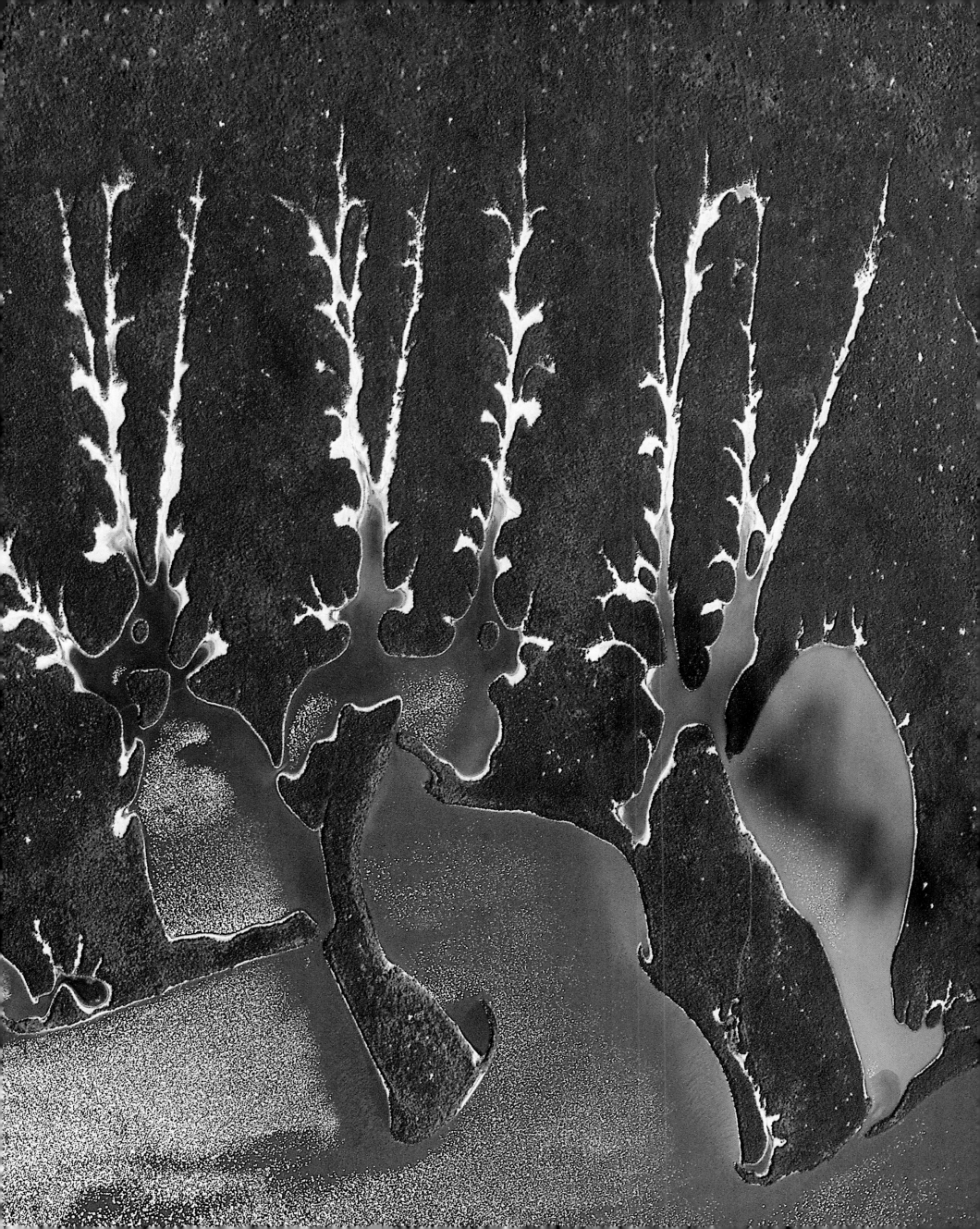

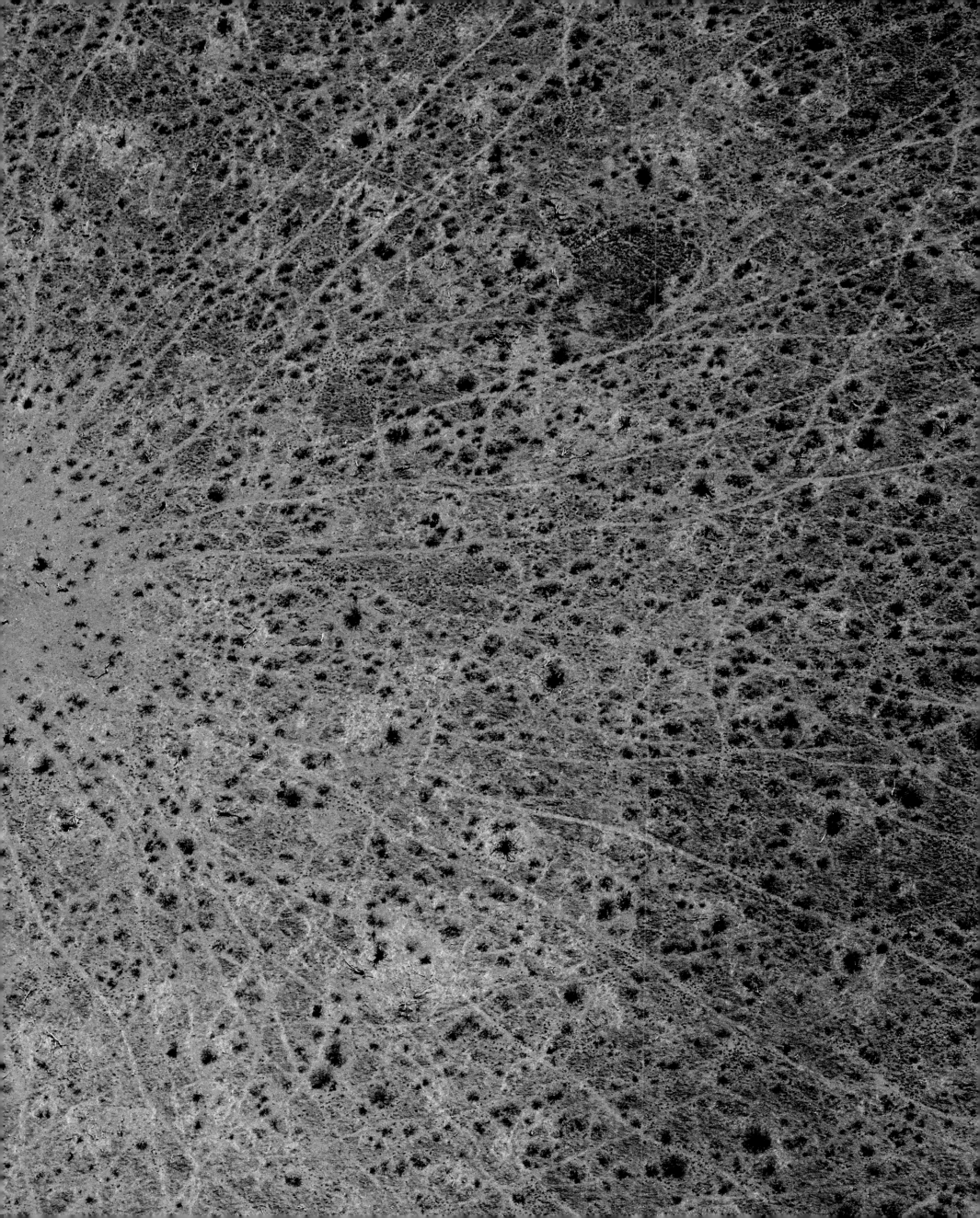

TRACES, RUINS, MEMORY

The existence of traces signifies that humans are at once "geographic" beings who engrave (*graphein*, from the Greek) the earth (*ge*) in the course of their existence, leaving signs of their activity wherever they go, as well as "historic" beings because of the way time past is taken into account by new generations. Objects from the past, removed from the sites where they were preserved, fill museums. The places of the past, reutilized or simply abandoned to the state of ruin, form part of the patrimony that our era will pass down to future generations. Are these ruins anything other than the sometimes incomprehensible traces of human activity? Are they witnesses for history? Yes—they constitute reference points, reminders in the life of present populations, useful elements for measuring time. In history there is always something "before," slightly more erased than what comes "after," far less known, more tenuous, and always incomplete. But who would dare say that a ruin is of no significance, of no importance? There is every reason, on the contrary, to value it and what can be made of it by us and by those who will succeed us.

TEMPORAL REFERENCE POINTS

Every human society transforms its environment, but until the twentieth century this action remained basically unconscious: no civilization before our own technological culture has ever imagined that it could have a palpable effect on the environment. Any thinker who dared express such a

---

p. 128
RESIDENCES ON AN ISLAND IN THE NIGER RIVER,
between Gourem and Gao, Mali
The Niger River winds among the sands in constant progression south of the Sahara, creating a large loop in Mali called the "camel's hump" by local people. After the rainy season, during periods of high water (from August to January), it floods vast expanses. Left above water are only a few small islets, called *toguéré*, which are sometimes inhabited. Although it occupies less than 15 percent of the Mali territory, the Niger River basin houses nearly 75 percent of the population, in addition to most of the country's metropolises. This river, which waters four countries in West Africa (Guinea, Mali, Niger, and Nigeria), reportedly takes its name from the Berber expression *gher-n-igheren*, which means "the river of rivers."

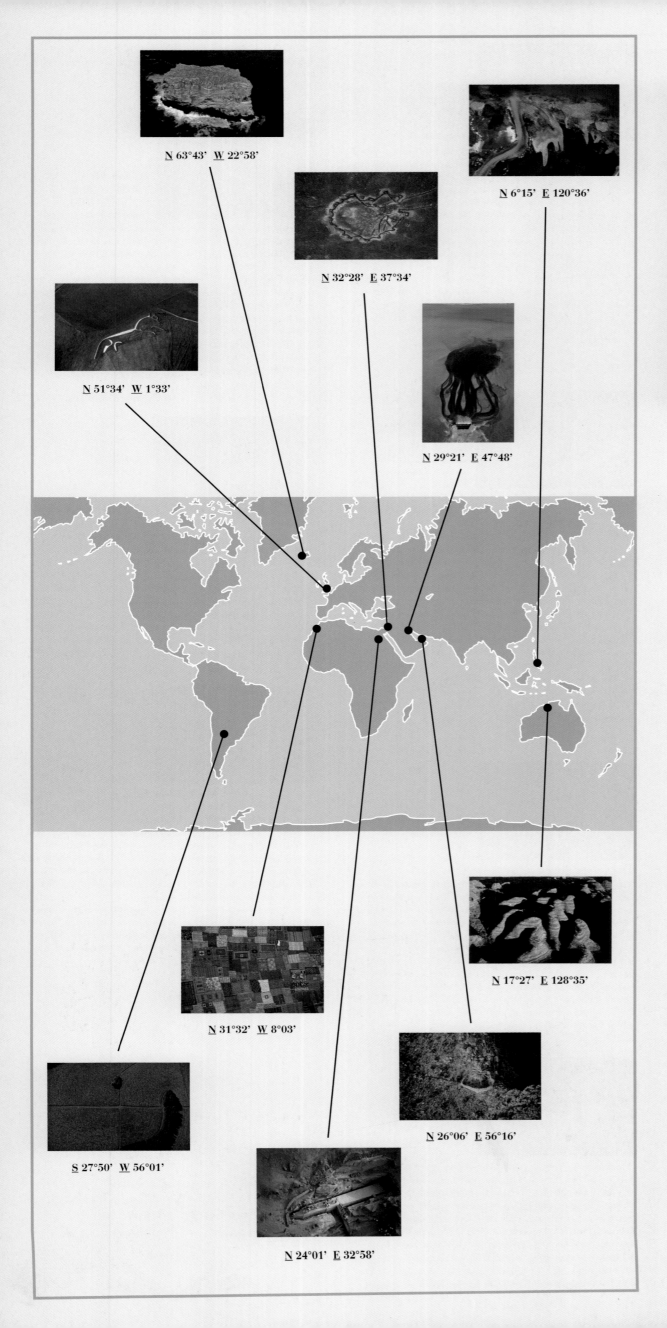

N 63°43' W 22°58'

N 6°15' E 120°36'

N 32°28' E 37°34'

N 51°34' W 1°33'

N 29°21' E 47°48'

N 17°27' E 128°35'

N 31°32' W 8°03'

N 26°06' E 56°16'

S 27°50' W 56°01'

N 24°01' E 32°58'

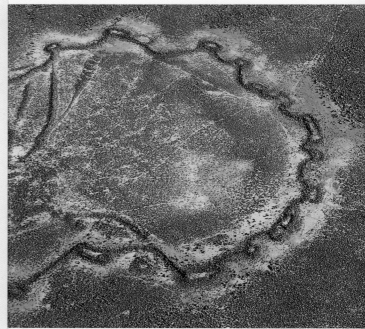

...ms, the incredible diversity of human ...n comparing those that have occupied ...different times.

...RRITORIES

...aphs do not show the original surface of ... societies throughout history have made ...r what the human eye can see of the pre- ...of its elements. Looking at these pho- ...help but note the ubiquity of industri- ... are surprised to discover traces of ...s where we would expect nature to have ...l human presence.

Terrestrial spaces before human
as nature made them (mountain, lal
and countless other classes of objects),
places. When they receive a population, o
tion of the soil, they are henceforth si
types of flux (fluxes of commerce, mig
munication). At that point they become
defined by their locations and the dista
but now also by their attributes—thei
forms assumed by the surface they occu
abstract vision is expressed "carnally"
landscapes.

Places and territories are defined
materiality—they are manipulated by u
but also mentally, as the object of sym
representation. Consequently, traces an
lizations enter into the consciousness of
among them today. Present-day societies

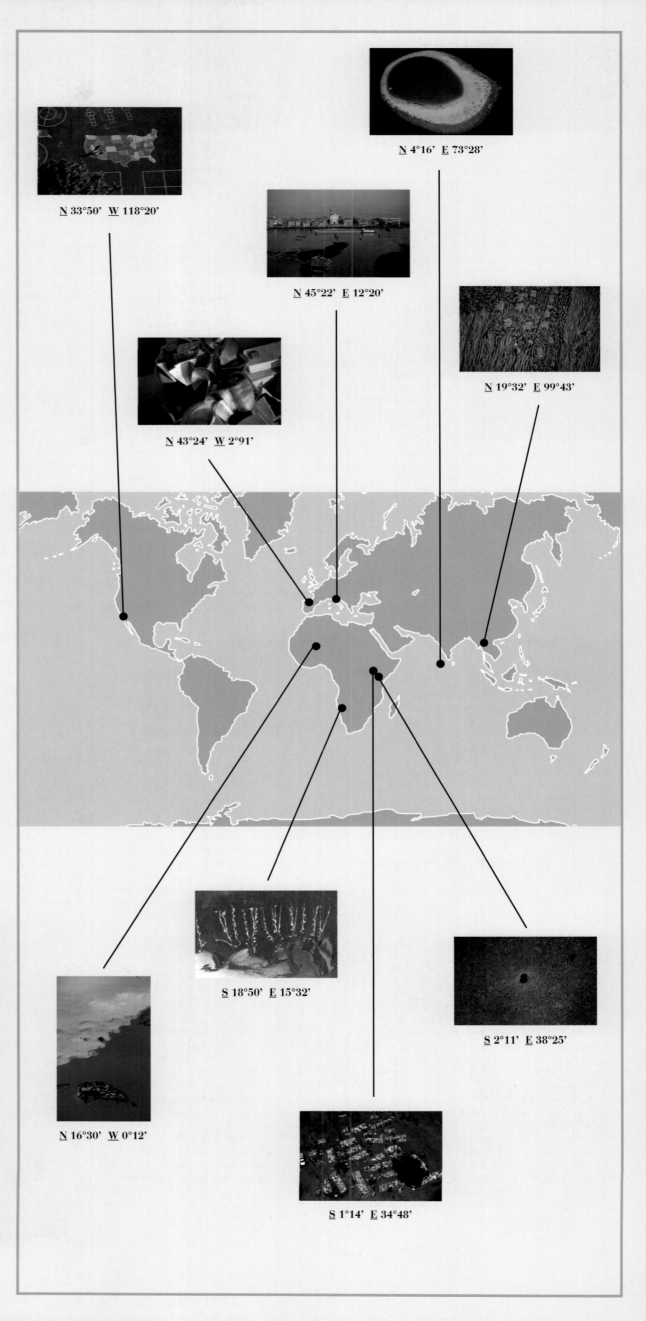

N 33°50' W 118°20'

N 4°16' E 73°28'

N 45°22' E 12°20'

N 19°32' E 99°43'

N 43°24' W 2°91'

S 18°50' E 15°32'

S 2°11' E 38°25'

N 16°30' W 0°12'

S 1°14' E 34°48'

of obsolete technologies to a world of hyperpowerful means.

The modern world never stops reusing ancient customs and, when it no longer understands them, reifying their elements. The result is a profusion of archaeological restorations and the accumulation of art objects in museums. Modern humanity imposes a multiplicity of viewpoints onto the constructions of the past, which serve not only as a basis for our pleasure but also as a springboard for our reflection. "Natural" spaces are subject to the creation of natural parks, reserves, defensive habitats, prohibitions against building, and interventions by landscapers commissioned to restore landscapes in the same manner that a plastic surgeon reconstructs a withered face.

Such protection requires recourse to government, and recent years have witnessed the preservation of spaces that have escaped the scars left by lines of communication and trade—a major sign, from city to city, of the expansion of present civilization. But this is not true everywhere. To ensure the global protection of ruins and landscapes of the past it is indispensable to appeal to a worldwide institution whose decisions will be respected.

Pierre Gentelle

---

p. 137
WASTE FROM A WATER DESALINATION PLANT
IN THE SEA OF AL-DOHA,
Jahra region, Kuwait
The two seawater desalination plants at Al-Doha in Kuwait produce 39,600 and 198,000 cubic feet (1,200 and 6,000 m³) of fresh water daily, using the instant thermal distillation technique (also known as the "flash" system). After treatment, water unfit for consumption is rejected into the sea or mixed with the waters of the Persian Gulf, creating the shape of a tentacled monster. For a long time Kuwait depended upon artesian wells and imports from Iraq for its supply of drinking water, but today it has several plants that produce more than 106 million gallons (400 million liters) of desalinated water per year, providing for 75 percent of the country's needs. Requiring enormous amounts of energy, the desalination stations are available only to states that have considerable resources, particularly petroleum, such as those in the Arabian peninsula. Featuring about 40 plants, this area produces more than half of the world's desalinated water.

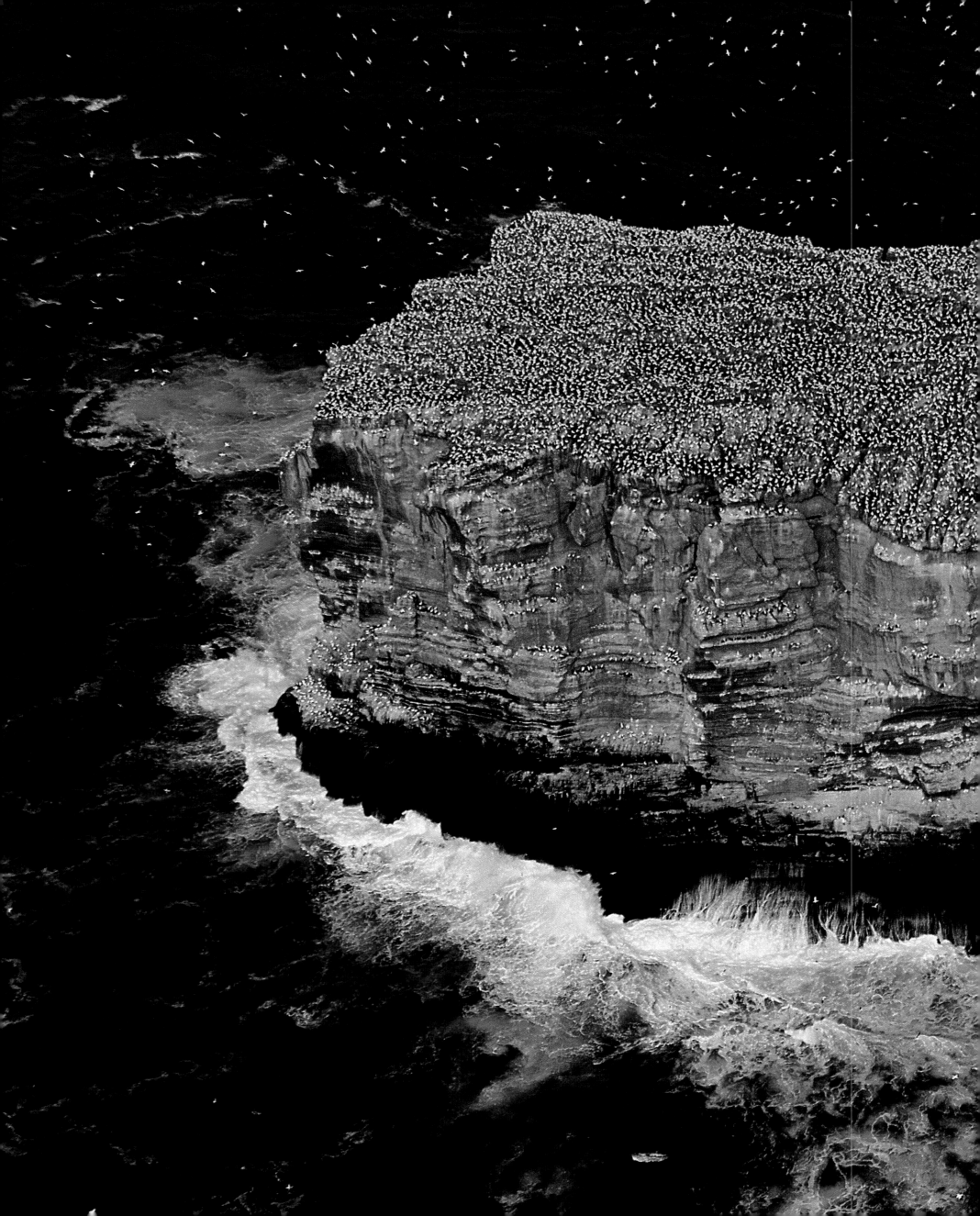

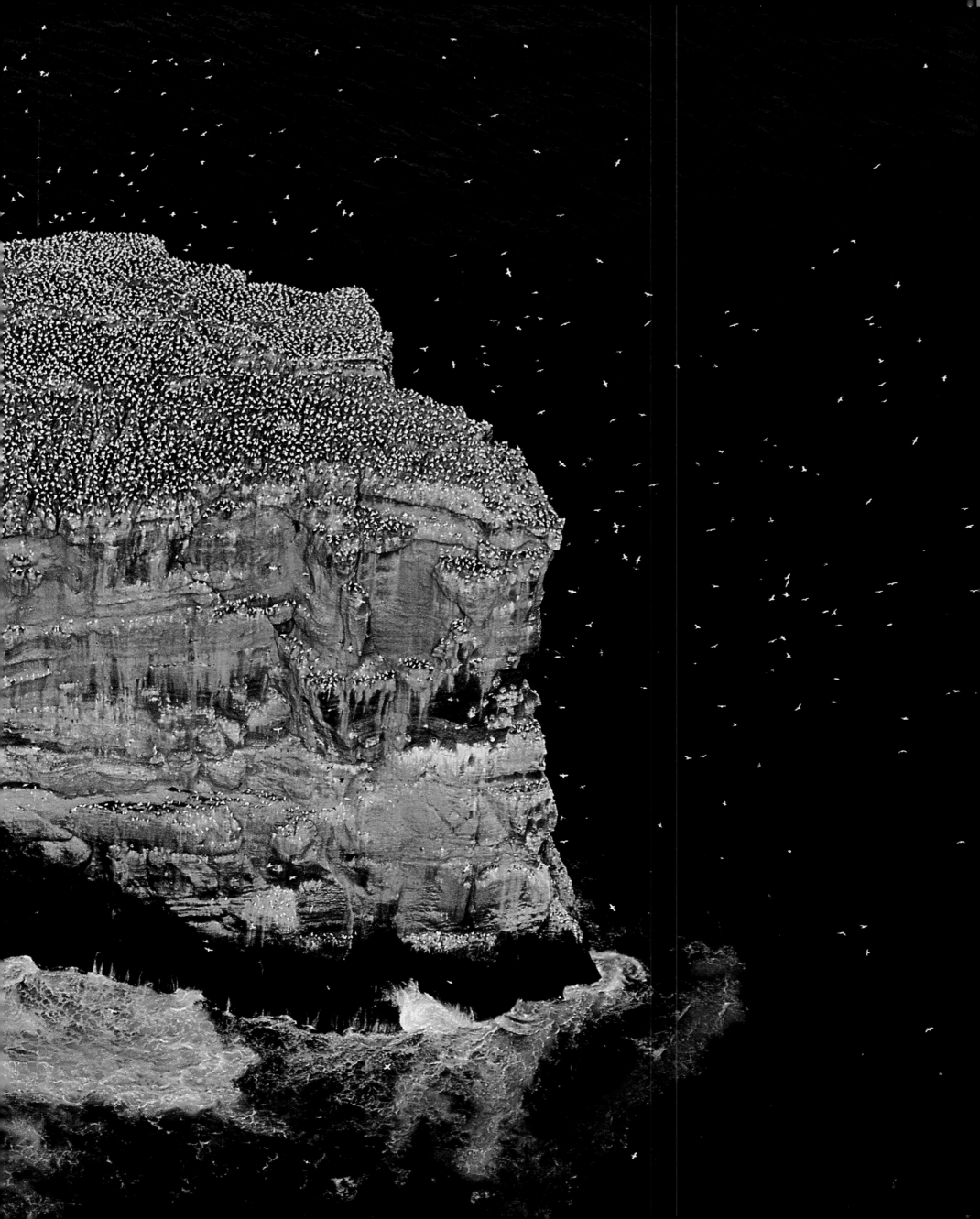

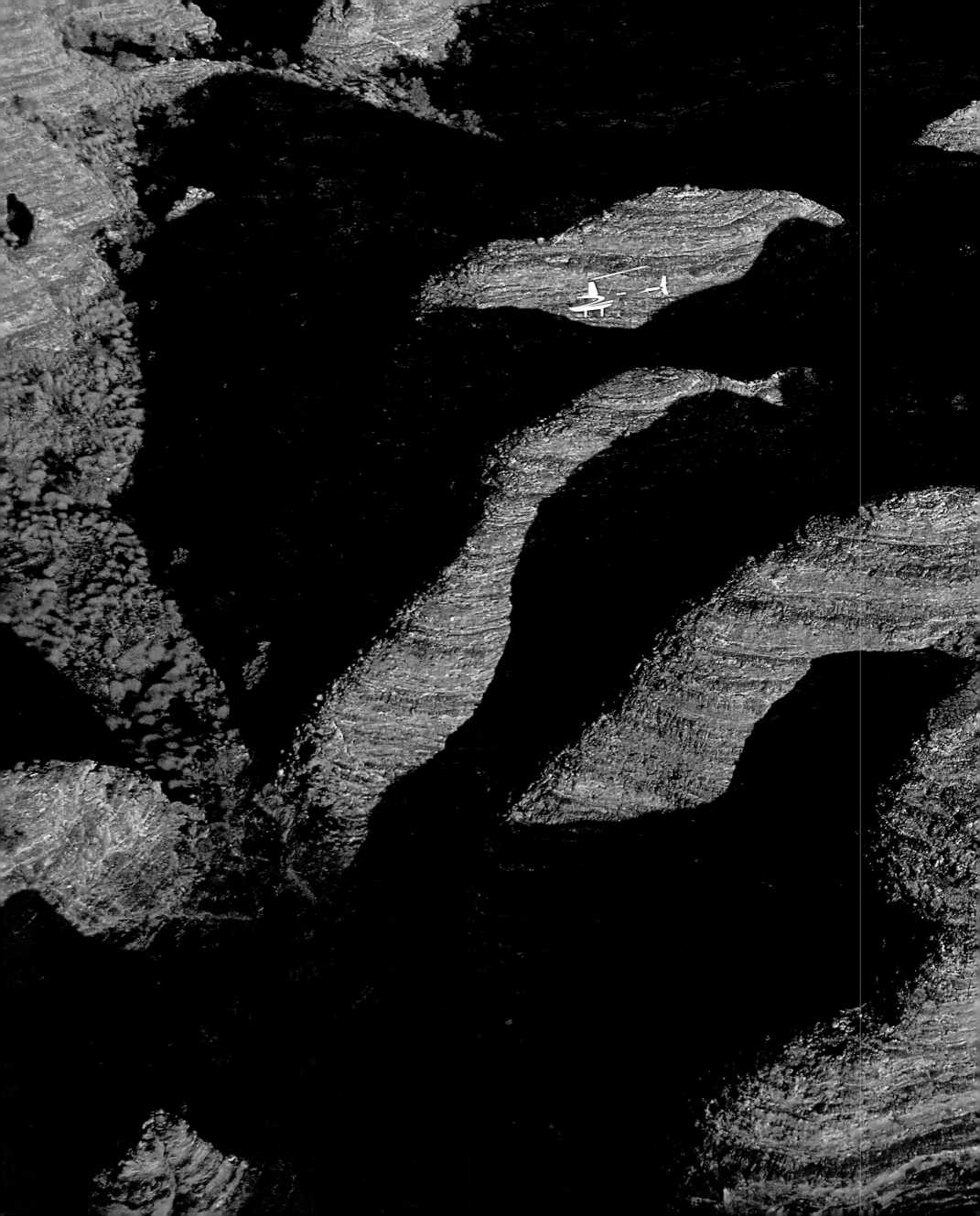

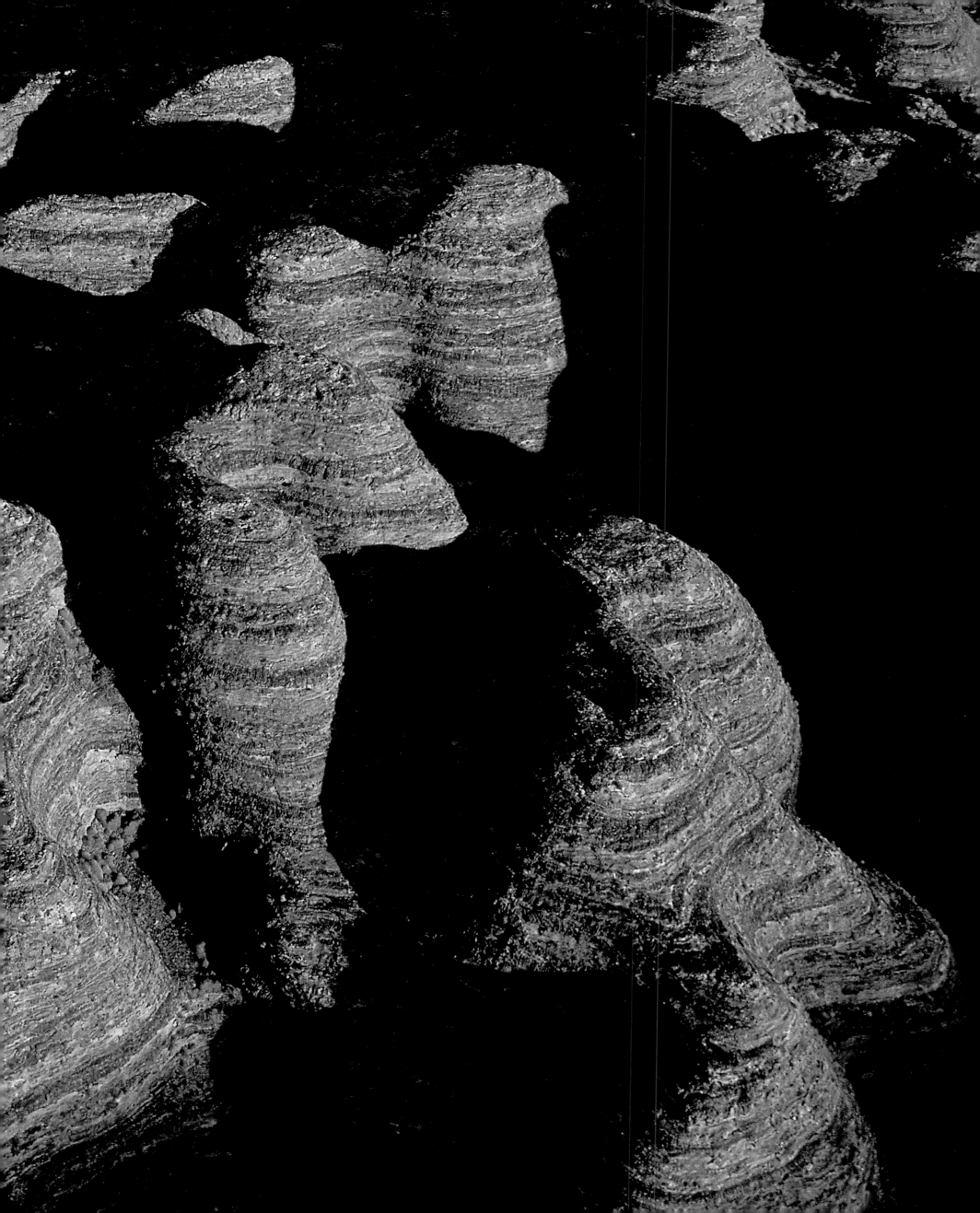

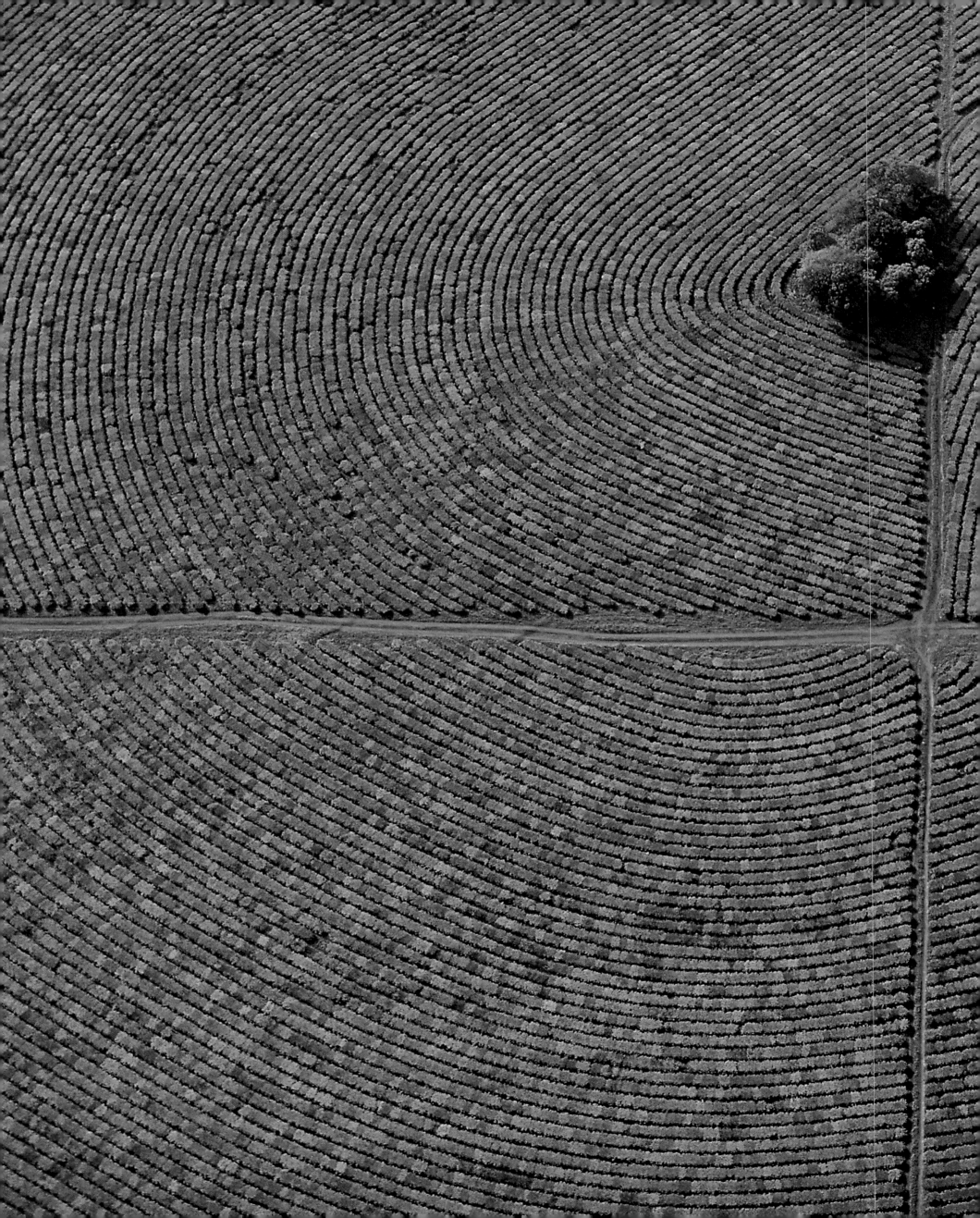

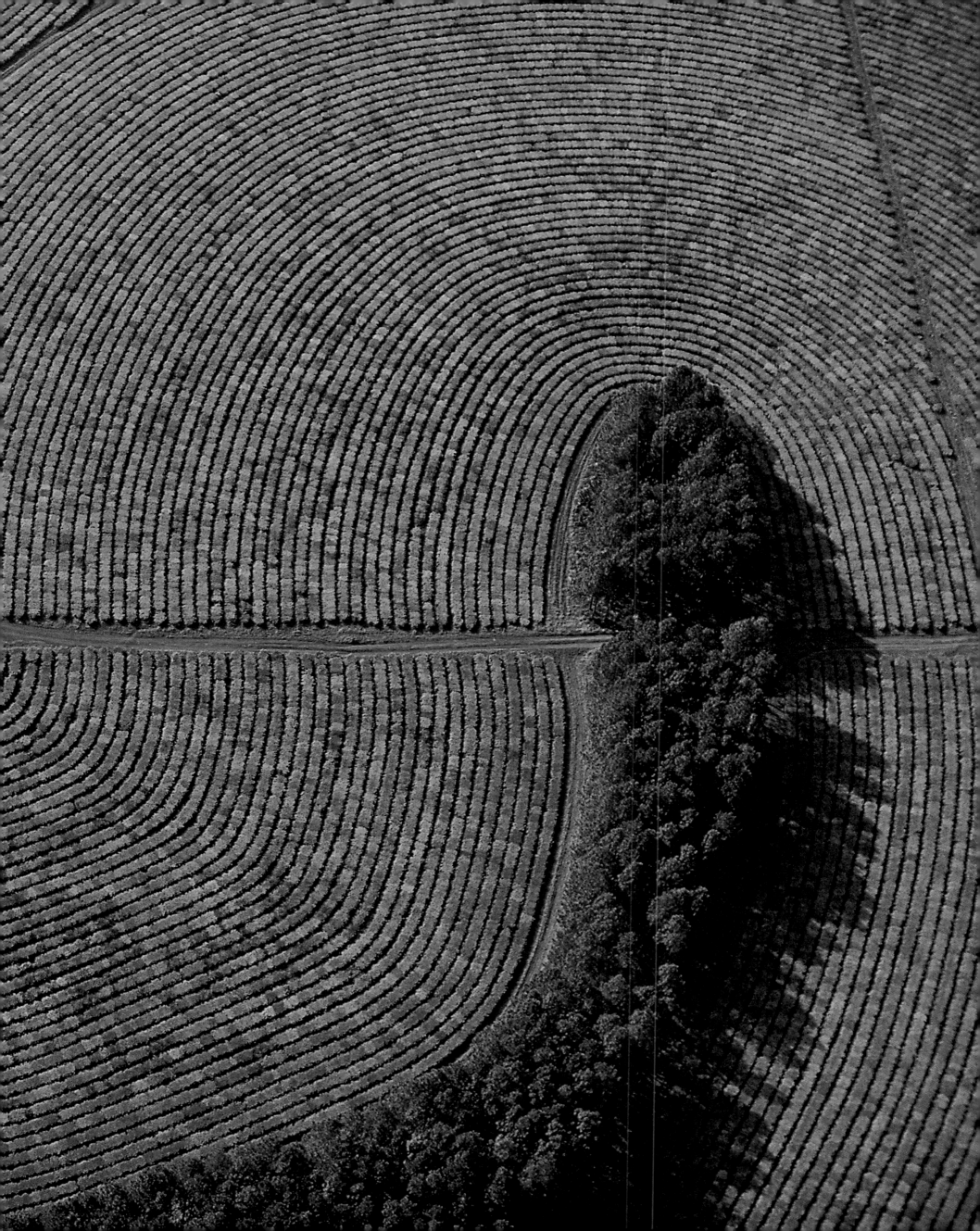

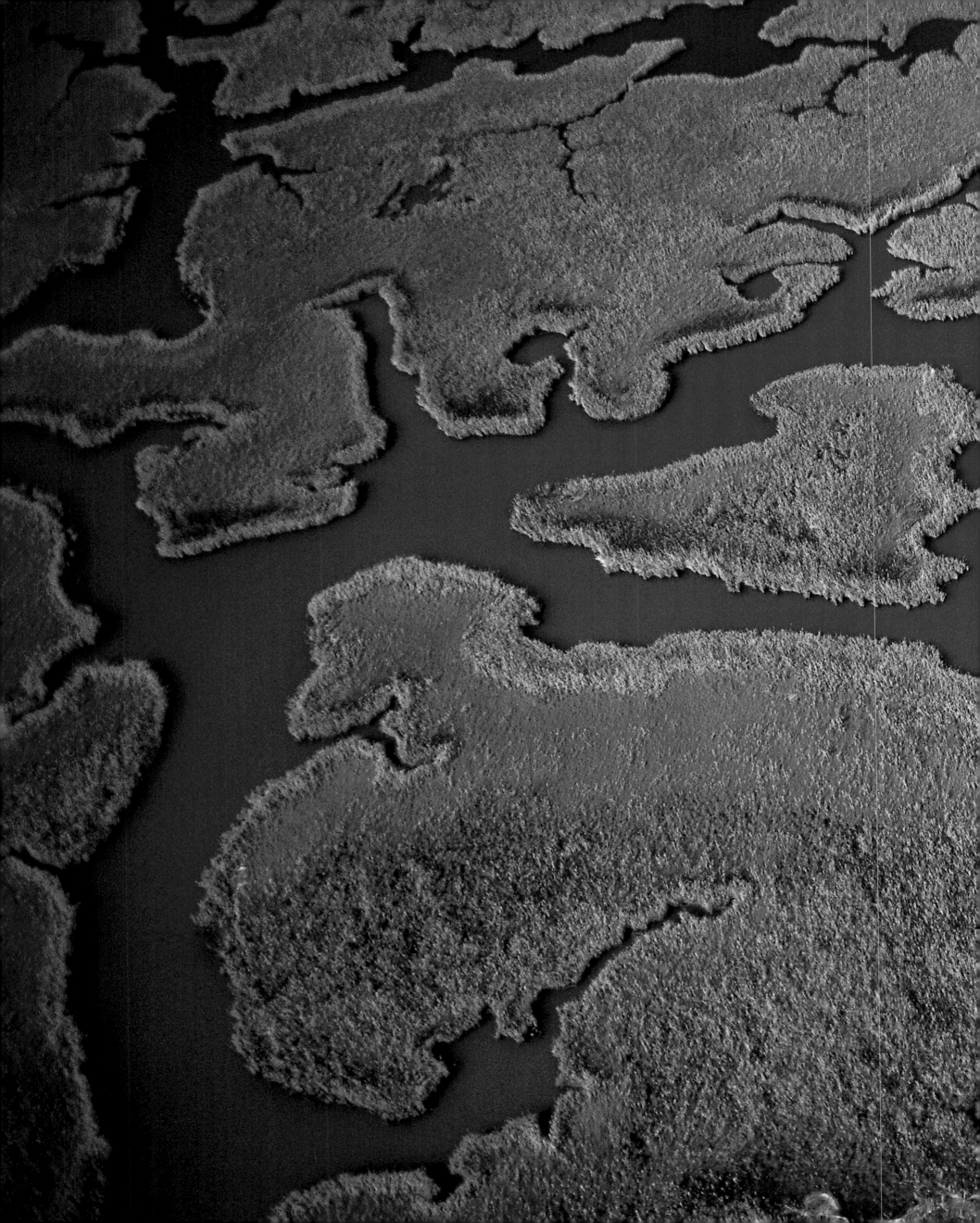

SPECTACLES AND LANDSCAPES

In the course of time, "human landscapes" have been constructed by societies. They represent the work of successive generations, completely different from "natural spectacles"—arrangements of natural objects such as rock, sea, sun, river, and beach. These are spectacles only for human beings, who view them and give them meaning; they are constructions of the human spirit. Human landscapes, on the other hand, are the product of the transformation of nature by the human species; they contain a portion of nature and a portion of "culture," or civilization. Created as much by the social organism itself as by its technologies and tools, these landscapes deserve to be called "landscapes of custom." They are linked to the way of life of a society, to the populations of its different segments (hamlet, village, burg, city, port) as well as to its relations with neighboring societies.

THE NATURAL LANDSCAPE AND THE IMAGINATION

Dictionaries remind us that the word *landscape* is no more than a few centuries old in the world's various languages, except in China, where evidence reports the use of a specific word starting in the fifth century A.D. The first paintings of landscapes were dedicated to rustic sites, and the

p. 168
PAVILIONS NEAR MIAMI,
Florida, United States
Famous for its beach tourism, Art Deco hotels, and luxury residences of movie stars, the city of Miami also contains residential suburbs with sober but comfortable pavilions. Built on former swampland that was dried up in the early twentieth century, these mushroom cities meet the demand of a population that keeps growing. Miami is located Dade County, a center of economic development, a place of refuge for exiles, and a favorite retreat for retirees. It has become the most densely populated region in Florida, claiming more than 2 million inhabitants. Florida was still largely wild at the beginning of the twentieth century but today, with a population of 14 million, it is the fourth-largest state in population. Its population has doubled in the past twenty years ago, and 85 percent live in urban areas.

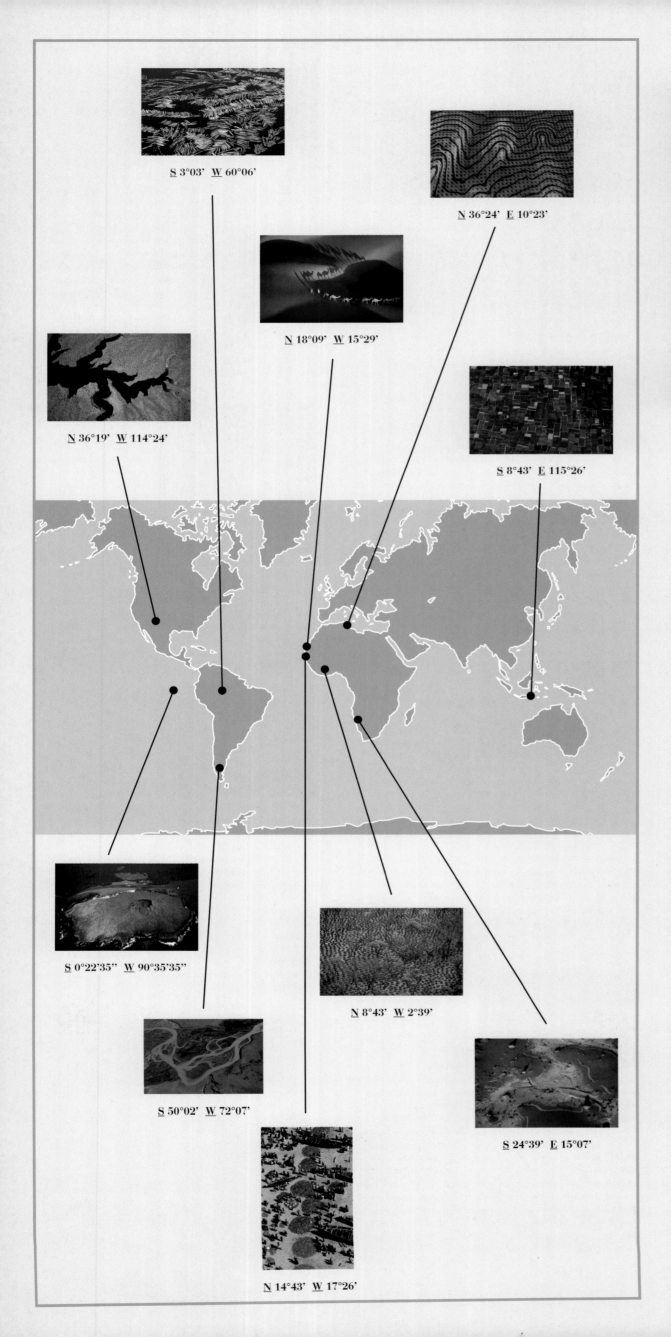

<u>S</u> 3°03' <u>W</u> 60°06'

<u>N</u> 36°24' <u>E</u> 10°23'

<u>N</u> 18°09' <u>W</u> 15°29'

<u>N</u> 36°19' <u>W</u> 114°24'

<u>S</u> 8°43' <u>E</u> 115°26'

<u>S</u> 0°22'35" <u>W</u> 90°35'35"

<u>N</u> 8°43' <u>W</u> 2°39'

<u>S</u> 50°02' <u>W</u> 72°07'

<u>S</u> 24°39' <u>E</u> 15°07'

<u>N</u> 14°43' <u>W</u> 17°26'

of gods reveals the powerlessness that the
confronted by nature. They were over-
they expressed this by imbuing nature
l force. The response of the inhabitants
ural landscapes stems from a quite dif-
re now powerful, but we experience a
n faced by a "simpler" world, a world
armony with nature. We take comfort in
at at one time we feared it. We may sense
of nature when we see a waterfall, but
moment in our life's experience.

re is a dreamlike magnification of every-
on our earth preceding mass production.
the nineteenth century was Neoclassical
g columns and spires, harking back to
d. The design aesthetic of the industrial

revolution was Art Nouveau, in which m
als and glass were shaped into organic
materials reconstructing the world they l

This makes it easier to understand t
quest conducted by those of our contem
ously seek out landscapes far removed f
place of residence, hoping to find purity a
and gentleness, silence and tenderness. T
ily accessible proximity of a nature that
industries, automobiles, and electric li
highly desirable by the very people who
ity and the internal combustion engine
rounded by industry.

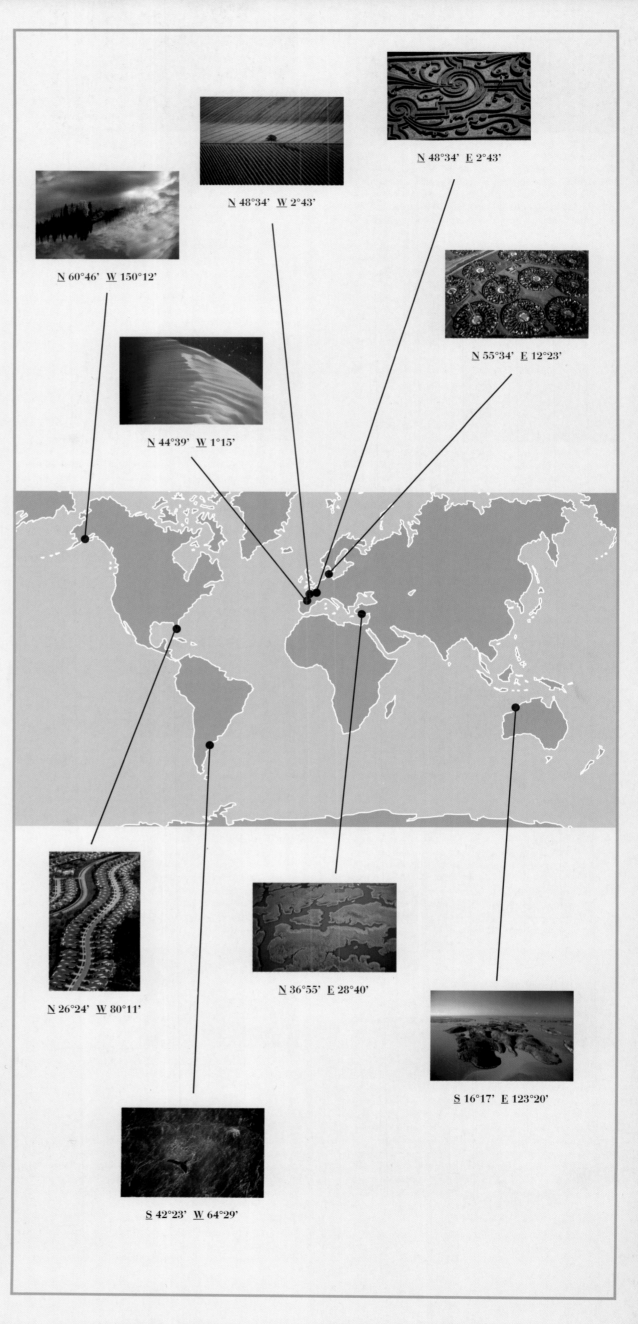

N 48°34' E 2°43'

N 48°34' W 2°43'

N 60°46' W 150°12'

N 55°34' E 12°23'

N 44°39' W 1°15'

N 26°24' W 80°11'

N 36°55' E 28°40'

S 16°17' E 123°20'

S 42°23' W 64°29'

Even measures taken to ensure the preservation of the "authentic" natural environment can end up by having a subversive effect. For instance, the creation of protected zones (such as natural parks and reserves) can signify tacit permission in other spaces to continue environmental exploitation. If the forest is safeguarded in one place, then it can be chopped down in another location. The separation—even opposition—between the human world and the natural world continues to grow, despite our increasing recognition of their interconnection. Untamed nature is thus tamed in these small, contained pockets; it is nature "quarantined," transformed into stage sets for humanity. In the modern world, authenticity is no longer possible.

Pierre Gentelle

p. 177
FISH MARKET NEAR DAKAR,
Senegal
The 435 miles (700 km) of the Senegalese coast benefit from a seasonal alternation between cool currents rich in minerals coming from the Canary Islands and warm equatorial currents. This makes the shoreline favorable to the development of rich and varied marine fauna. Fish resources are intensely exploited in this area, producing 360,000 tons annually. Eighty percent of the fishing is carried out from pirogues, dugout canoes of baobab or kapok trees, using lines or nets. The fish, Senegal's chief economic resource, mainly goes to the local market; tuna, sardines, and cod are sold right off the beach at the landing points of the pirogues. In Senegal, as in most developing countries, fish provides 40 percent of the protein consumed by the population.

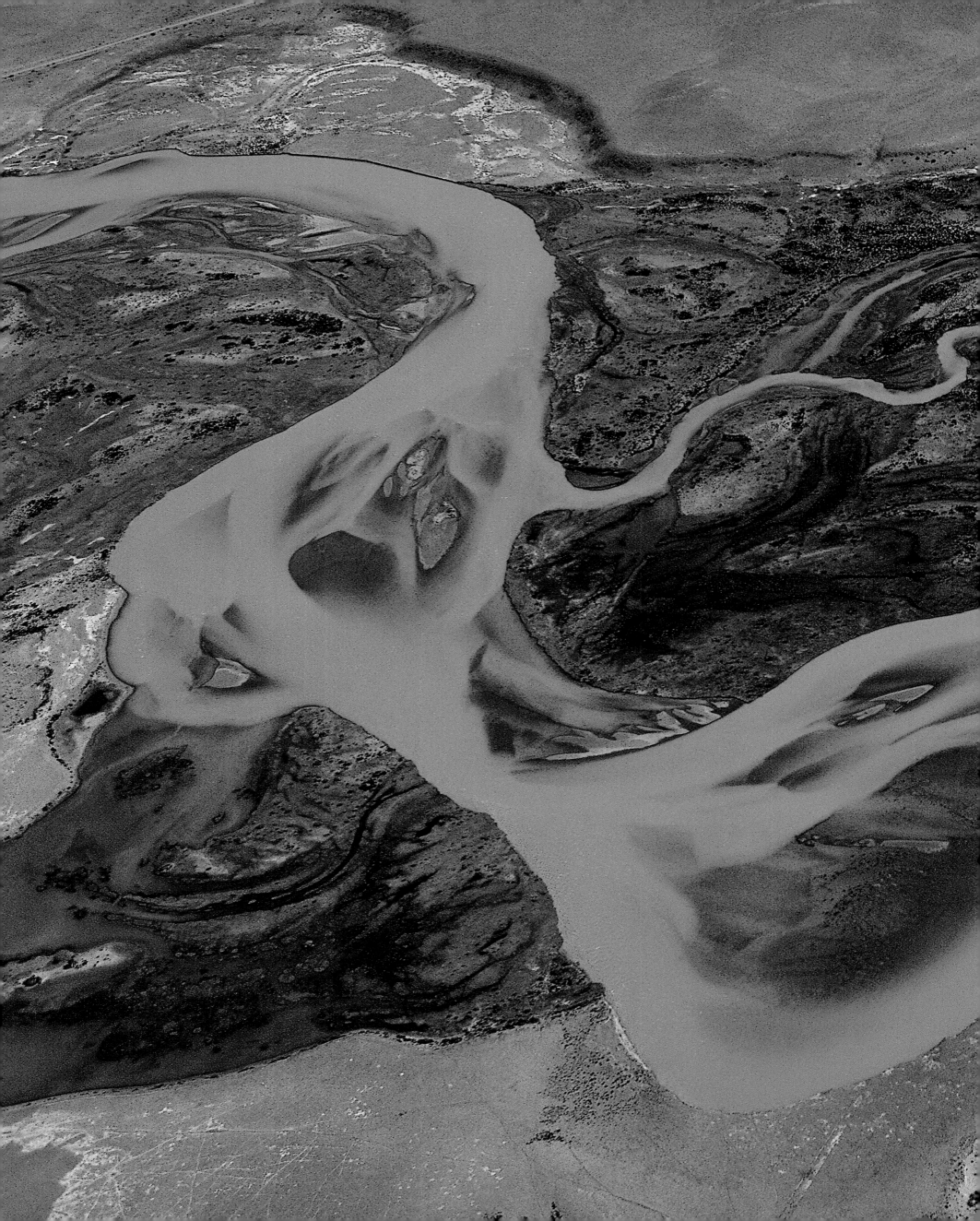

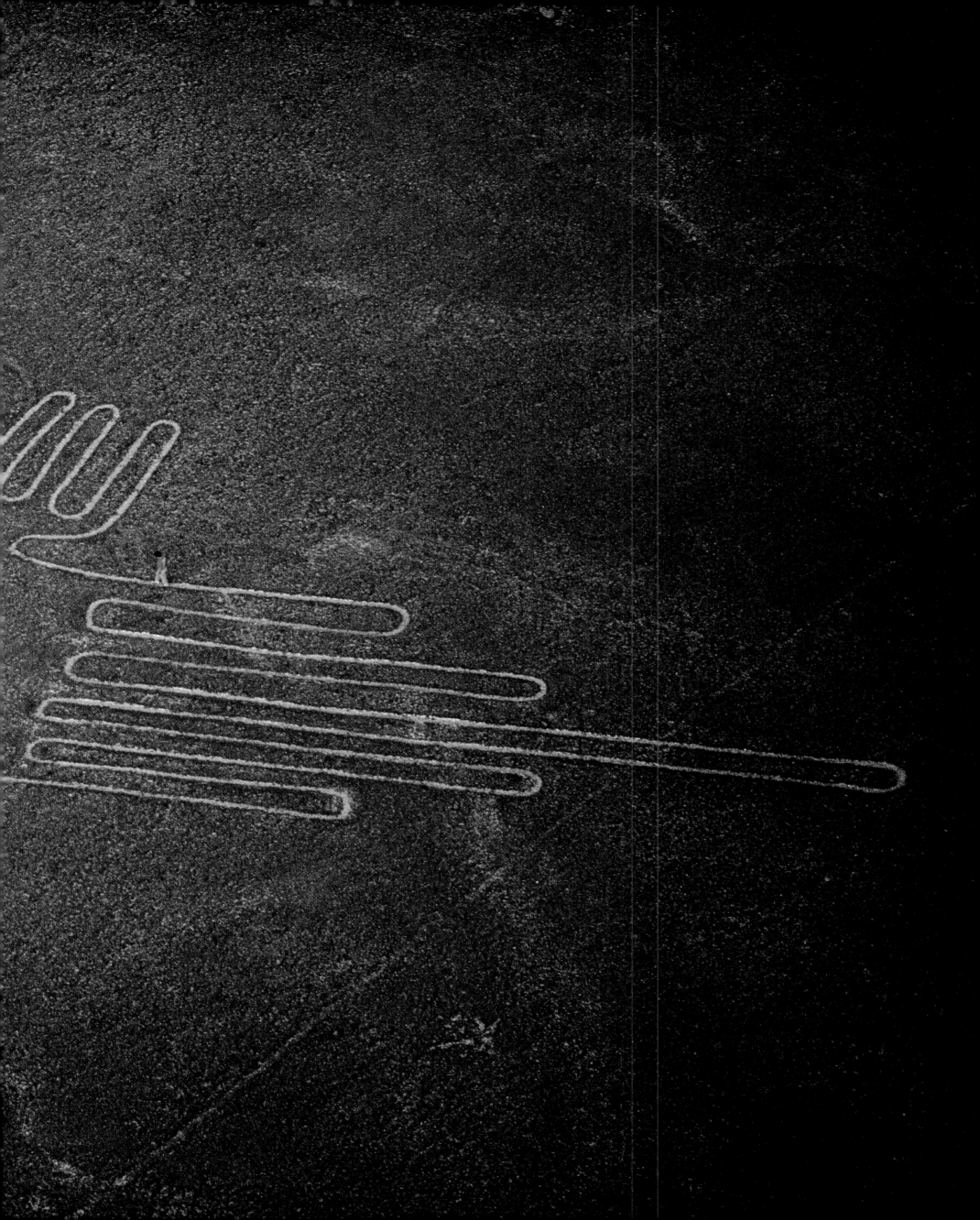

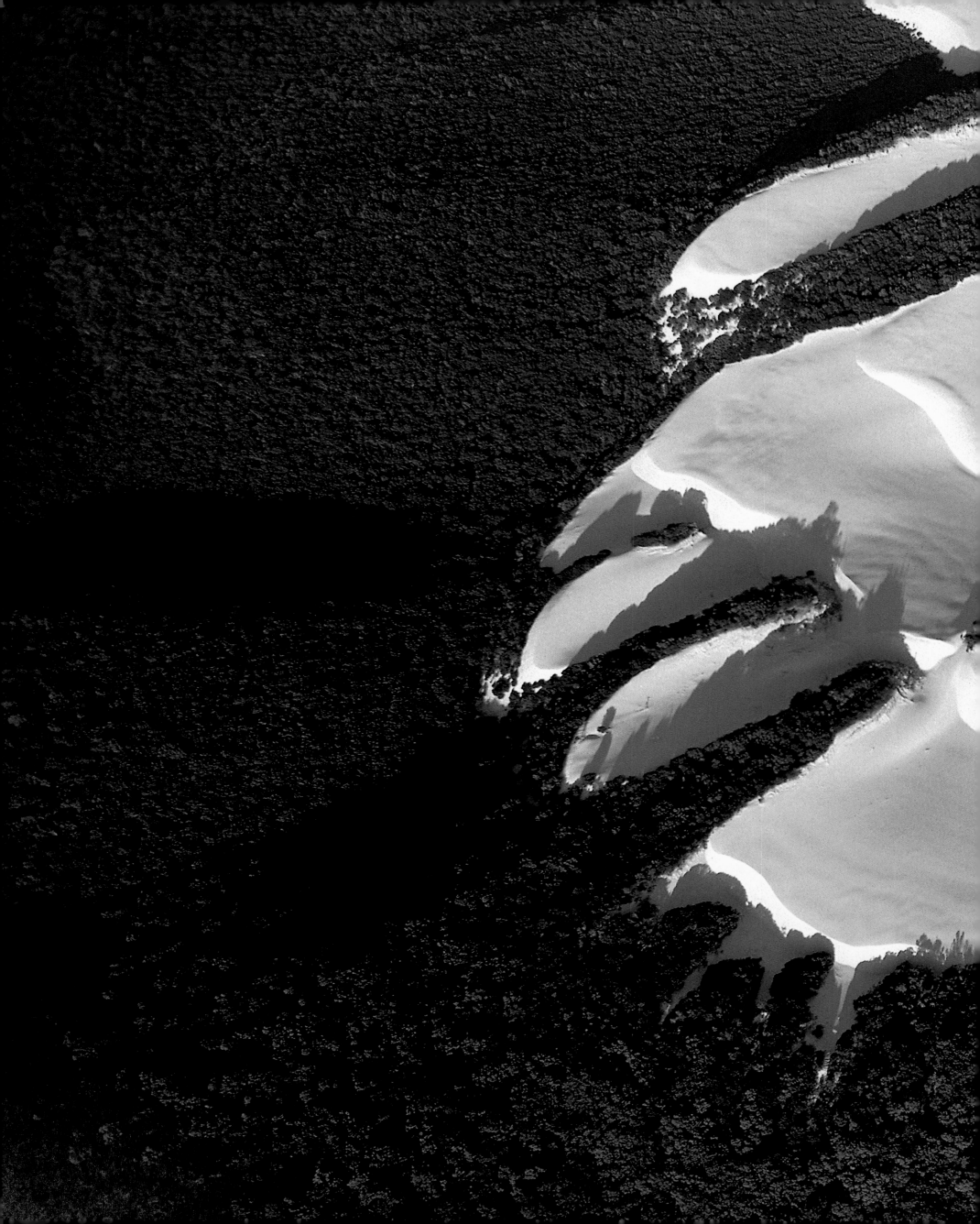

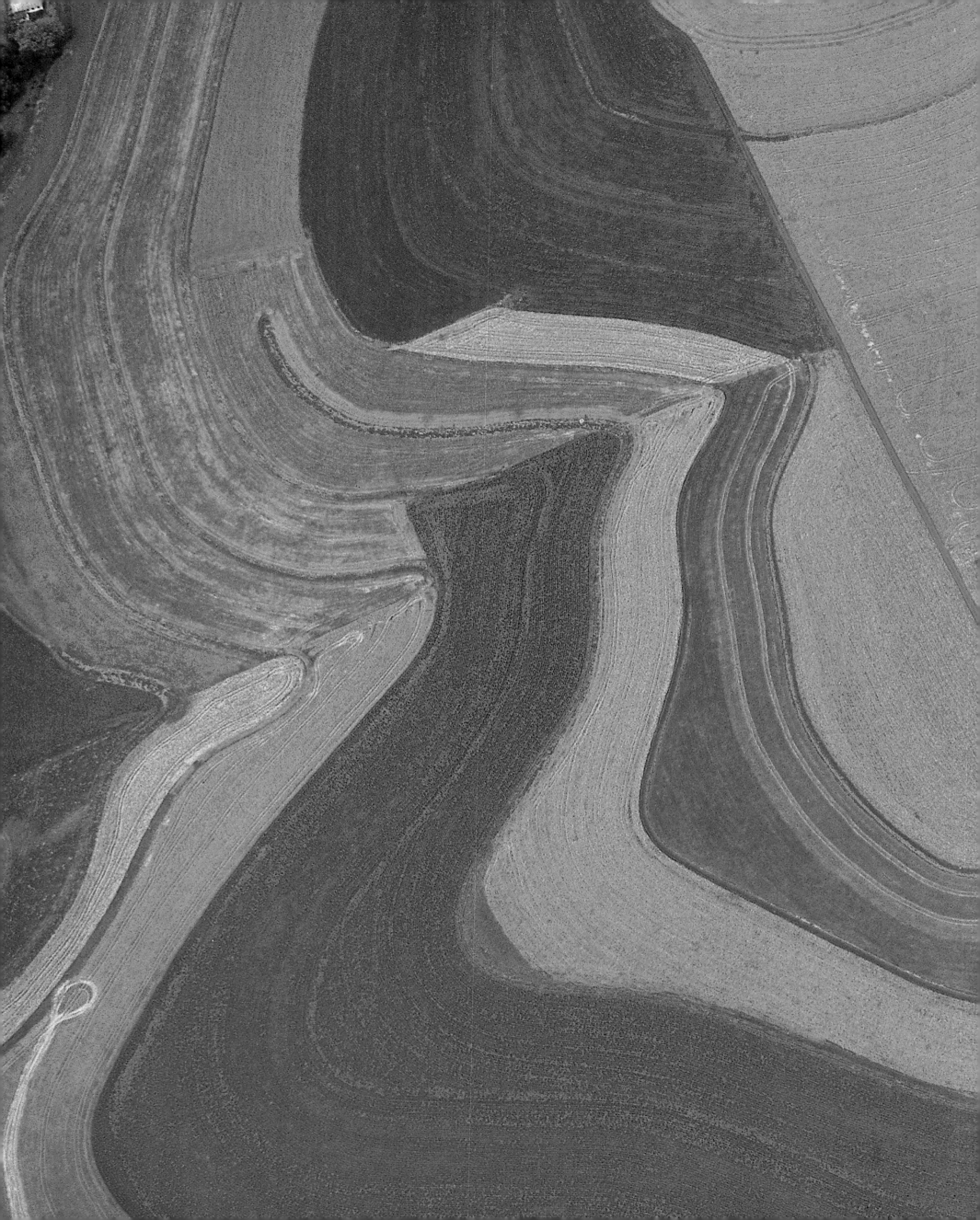

FUTURE OF THE CITY, FUTURE OF LIFE

What is a city? It is, spatially, the unity of a multiplicity. It shares this quality, in social or mental terms, with a society or an idea. Thus, through its urban, political, and intellectual constructs, humanity adapts the complexities of the universe to its own needs. At the dawn of the twenty-first century, however, the city is experiencing a crisis. We see the city fragment even as it proliferates; society is torn apart, while the population grows as never before. Is the city evolving or devolving?

---

p. 208
TOURISTS ON A BEACH AT FUERTEVENTURA, near Corralejo,
Canary Islands, Spain
Fuerteventura, the second largest of the Canary Islands, has the most expansive beaches of the entire archipelago. Taking advantage of one of many isolated inlets, these tourists are enjoying the pleasures of nudity and full-body tanning. No doubt inspired by the practice of local farmers, they have built a low wall of volcanic stone as protection from the winds from the Sahara that continually sweep the coast, to the great joy of wind surfers. Fuerteventura was selected as the site for the largest hotel complex in the world, but the island's shortage of freshwater, a problem for nearly 20 percent of the population of the archipelago, quickly caused the ambitious project to be dropped. Tourism nevertheless remains the chief industry of the Canaries, which receive 4 million visitors each year, 97 percent of whom come from Germany.

UNITY AND MULTIPLICITY

The question is crucial: how shall we model the city and an increasingly urban society? To seek an answer, let us review the film of the city's history. Perhaps we will then be in a better position to detect, in the current upheaval, what is a danger for the future and what is an opportunity to be grasped.

Approximately one hundred thousand years ago our ancestors began to colonize the planet in groups of twenty or thirty, moving about while hunting and gathering. Then, about ten thousand years ago, some of them settled in one place, inventing agriculture and the village. All of these communities, and all of the individuals who constituted them (aside, of course, from certain distinctions based on gender and age), carried out the same activities.

Diversification was created by the city, through the division of labor. A new form of social organization, reciprocal yet hierarchical, was born: at the bottom the producers, above them the warriors, and at the top the sovereign, a power

209

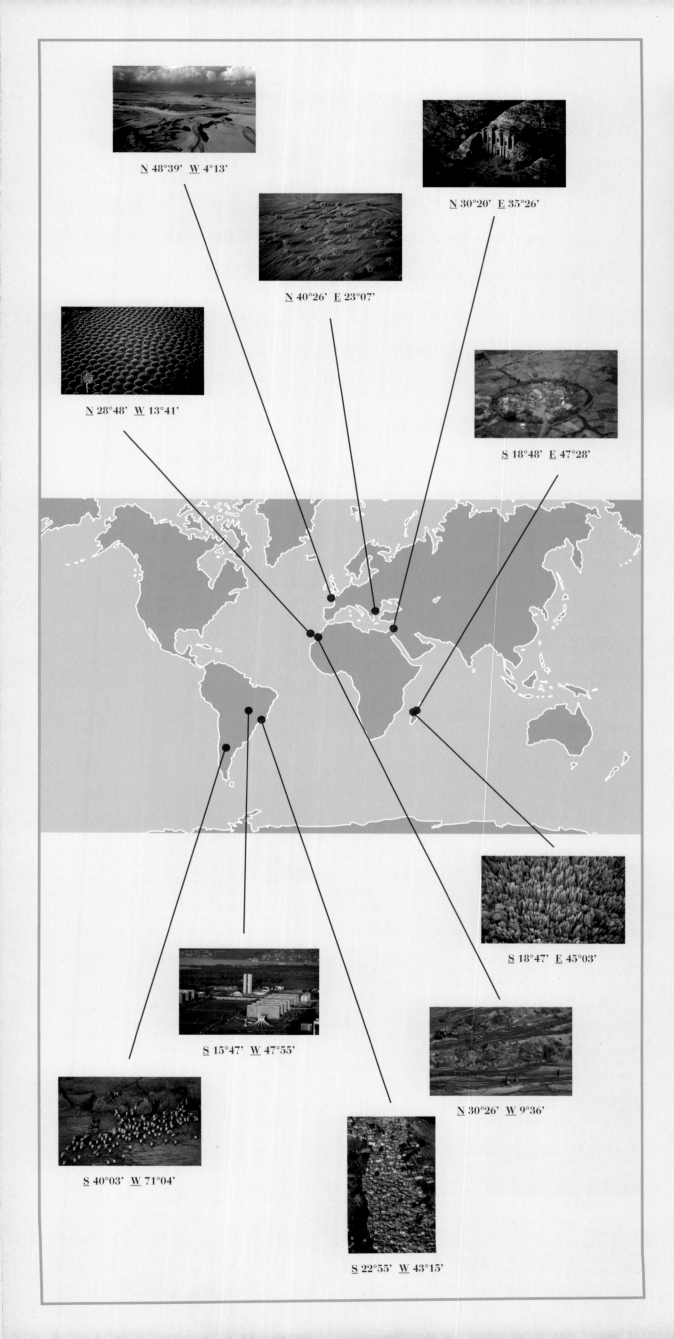

N 48°39' W 4°13'

N 30°20' E 35°26'

N 40°26' E 23°07'

N 28°48' W 13°41'

S 18°48' E 47°28'

S 18°47' E 45°03'

S 15°47' W 47°55'

N 30°26' W 9°36'

S 40°03' W 71°04'

S 22°55' W 43°15'

birth to the modern city. It was released

res by classical Greece and especially

Neolithic village by the medieval city of

e Paris of the kings of France, emblem-

disassociates itself from the religious, and

with its powerful dynamism that trans-

re like to say, are marked by the spirit of

osophy separates the infinite extension of

nking subject. The former became homo-

le, and the subject made itself the mas-

f the material world through science, by

try. The king was the master of his realm,

on to flatten and square off his territory,

"French garden." Recall the Paris of the

nteenth centuries, its Place Royale, which

les Vosges: identical buildings arranged

closing in its center the equestrian statue

war leader. The manifestation of power

precision symbolized militarization, epit-

omized by the similar layout of the Invali[des]
complex in Paris, with Napoleon's tomb [at]
the sides of the quadrilateral, all of soci[ety]
its king; and, from his central position, t[he]
society in his haughty gaze.

Thus, the city made society a great [...]
lated by techno-engineers (such as the M[...]
the military engineer whose tactics and in[...]
sible Louis XIV's wars, and Jean-Baptist[e...]
ister of finance who oversaw the acade[my of]
the arts). Normalization and academicism[...]
with social controls. This model, which w[...]
places, such as St. Petersburg, posited a un[...]
nal, creative diversity. Here was an inert [...]
"scientific" administration engendered s[...]

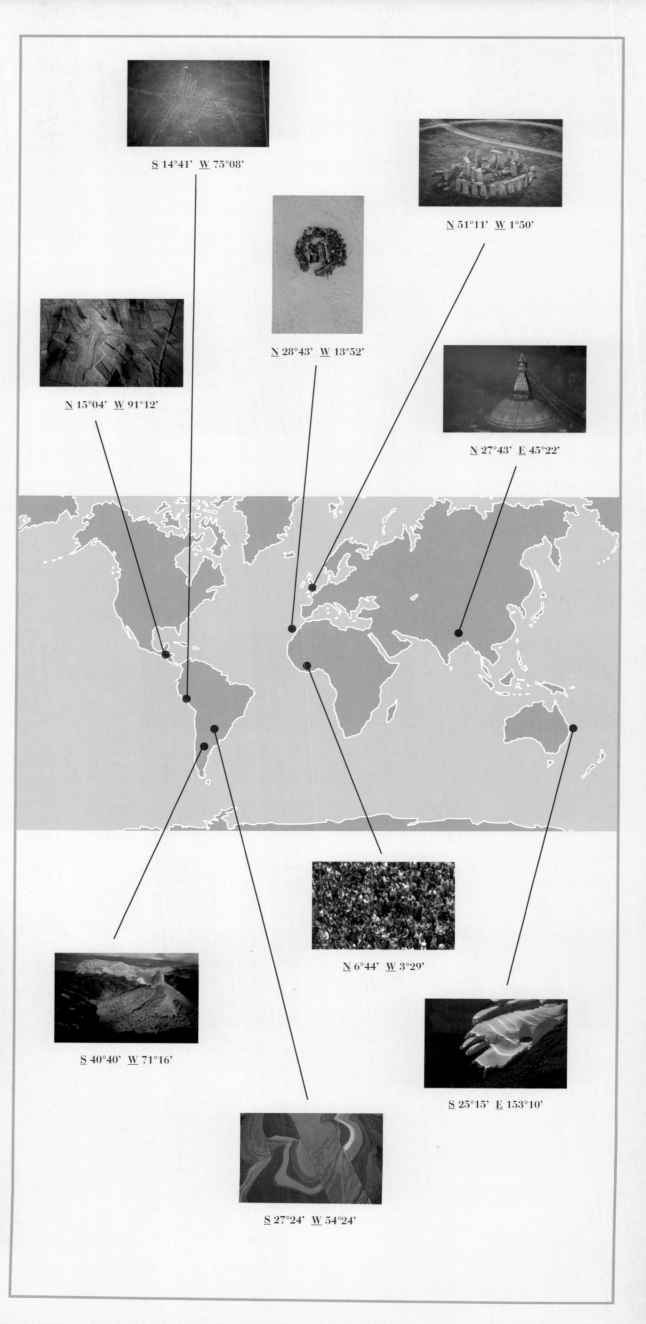

S 14°41' W 75°08'

N 51°11' W 1°50'

N 28°43' W 13°52'

N 15°04' W 91°12'

N 27°43' E 45°22'

N 6°44' W 3°29'

S 40°40' W 71°16'

S 25°15' E 153°10'

S 27°24' W 54°24'

and circulation, the industrial city made its distinctions completely visible and kept its denizens enslaved to this machine that heats, smokes, and floods the market with its products. Everything, including sexual energy, was co-opted, disciplined for work, manipulated for consumption. Life was reduced to one dimension, entirely instrumentalized. This means of unifying differences, far from complicating the human being, reduced it to material production alone.

And yet today there is a certain nostalgia for these figures of the past. This is because urban life is exploding before our eyes: forty-five percent of the population of the planet now lives in cities, some of which are becoming gigantic. In the developing nations of Latin America, Africa, South and Southeast Asia, over thirty cities have more than 5 million inhabitants. As the global marketplace unifies world trade, it anarchizes the cities. In the developing world, conglomerates are overtaking traditional agriculture, and the rural population is swarming to the cities. While the periphery spreads at a galloping rate, the former city disintegrates in its very center: city centers are lost in the city sprawl, and the historical city dissolves into a new form.

Everywhere the old areolar, concentric structure is giving way to a networked fabric, as seen in cities such as Los Angeles and Mexico City. In the historical city, the State and the productive machine regulated the functioning of a precise territory. But today, due to the fluidity of capital and intelligence, these pillars of power and effectiveness have been undermined, leading to a proliferation of edge cities, which, unregulated, can degenerate into violence. Global-

ization might have been expected to lead to homogenization and standardization. In fact, it has given rise to societal dislocation.

A New Dynamic

It would be taking a pessimistic and conservative stance, however, to view today's cities as on the verge of complete collapse. What we see today as chaos is a new stage in urban development, a new dynamic. The absence of a firm city center does not have to spell the breakdown of authority and regulation. The network of the city is a reflection of democratic society, a combination of individualization and socialization, independence and community. The history of the city is important to keep in mind, but it should not blind us to the innovation and opportunities of the present.

Paul Blanquart

p. 217
FAVELAS IN RIO DE JANEIRO, Brazil
Nearly one-fourth of the 10 million cariocas—the residents of Rio de Janeiro—live in the city's 500 shantytowns, known as *favelas*, which have grown rapidly since the turn of the twentieth century and are wracked by crime. Primarily perched on hillsides, these poor, underequipped neighborhoods regularly experience fatal landslides during the heavy rain season. Meanwhile, downhill from the *favelas*, the comfortable middle classes of the city (18 percent of cariocas) occupy the residential districts along the oceanfront. This social contrast marks all of Brazil, where 10 percent of the population controls the majority of the wealth while nearly half of the country lives below the poverty level. Approximately 25 million Brazilians live in shantytowns in the nation's large metropolitan areas.

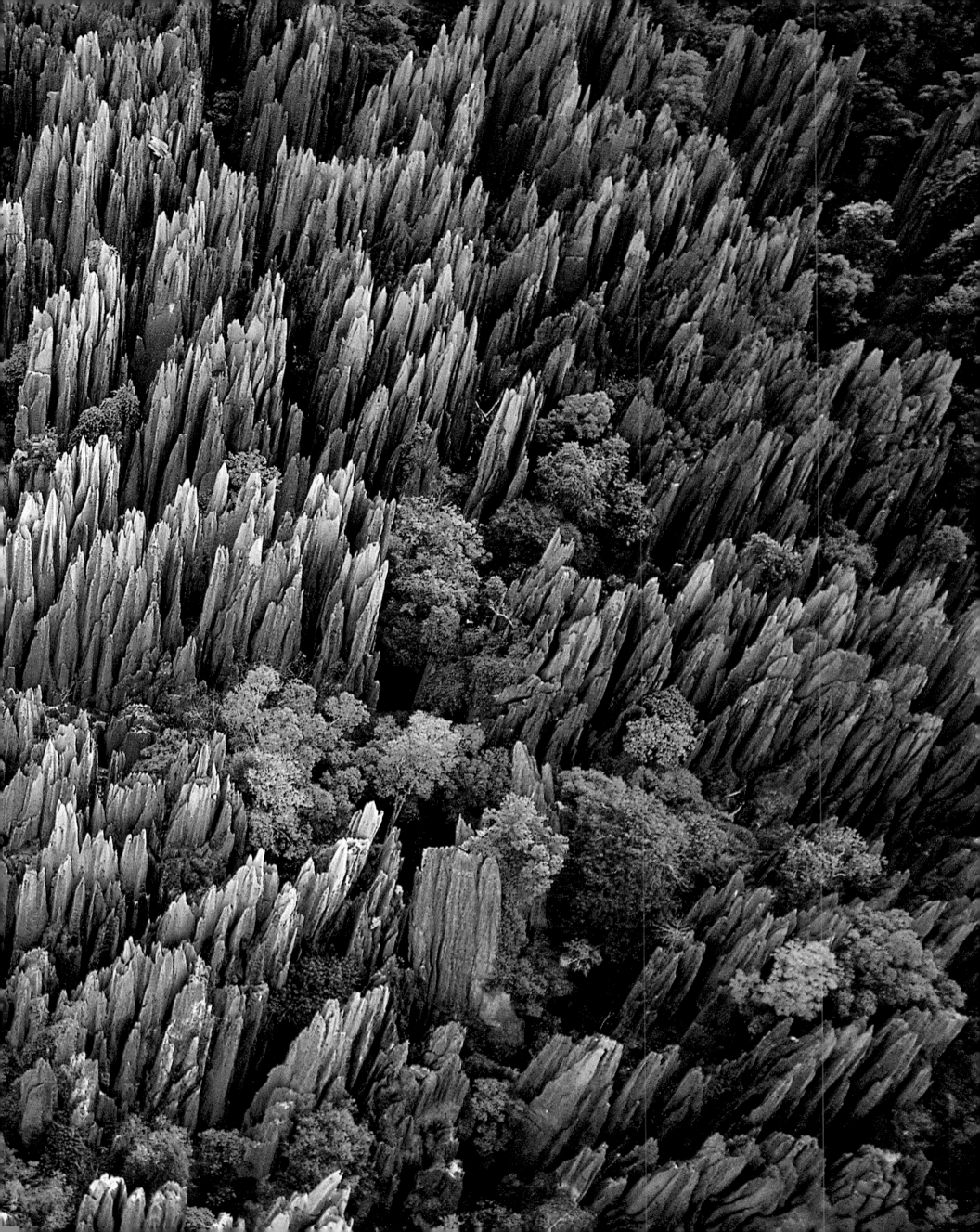

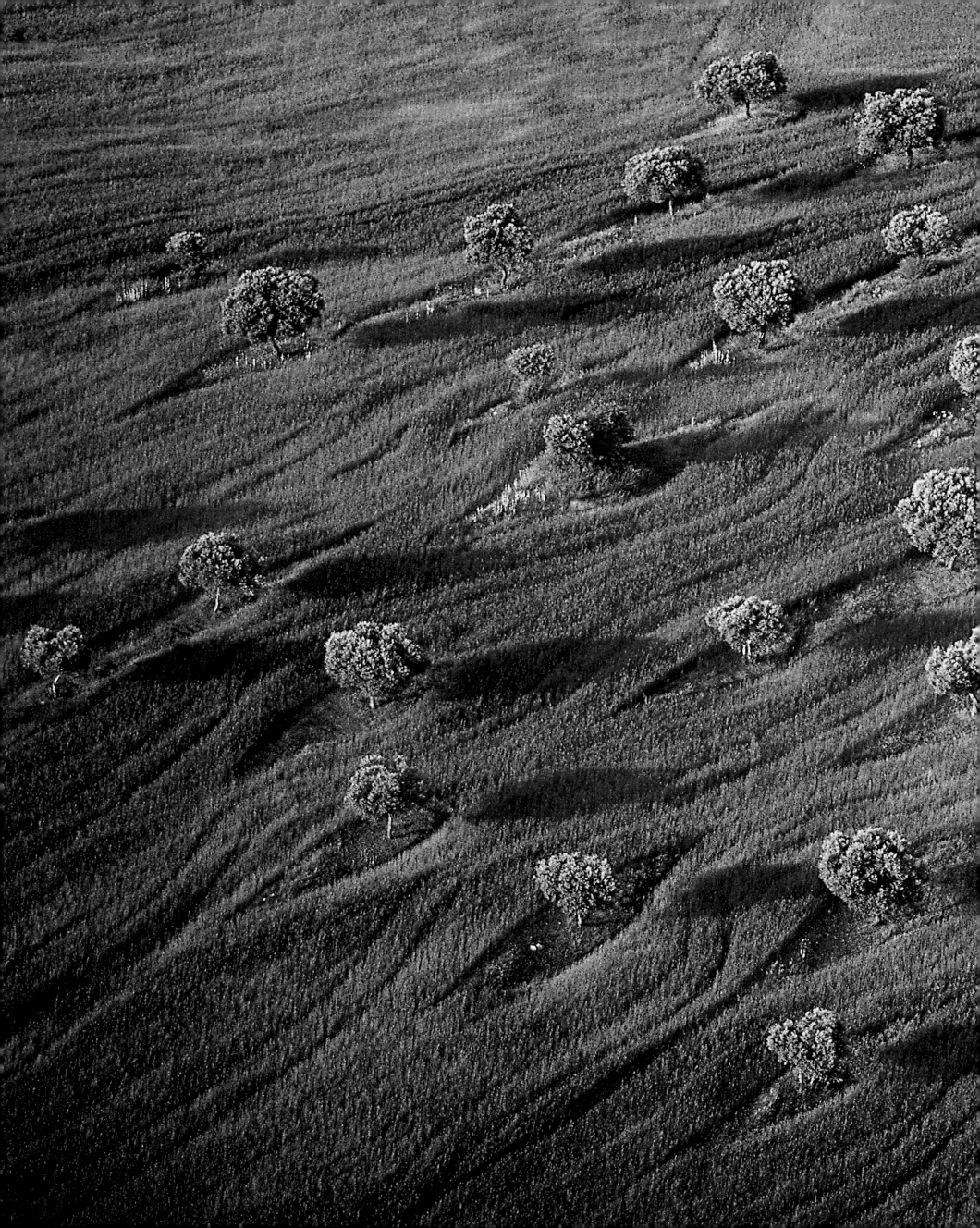

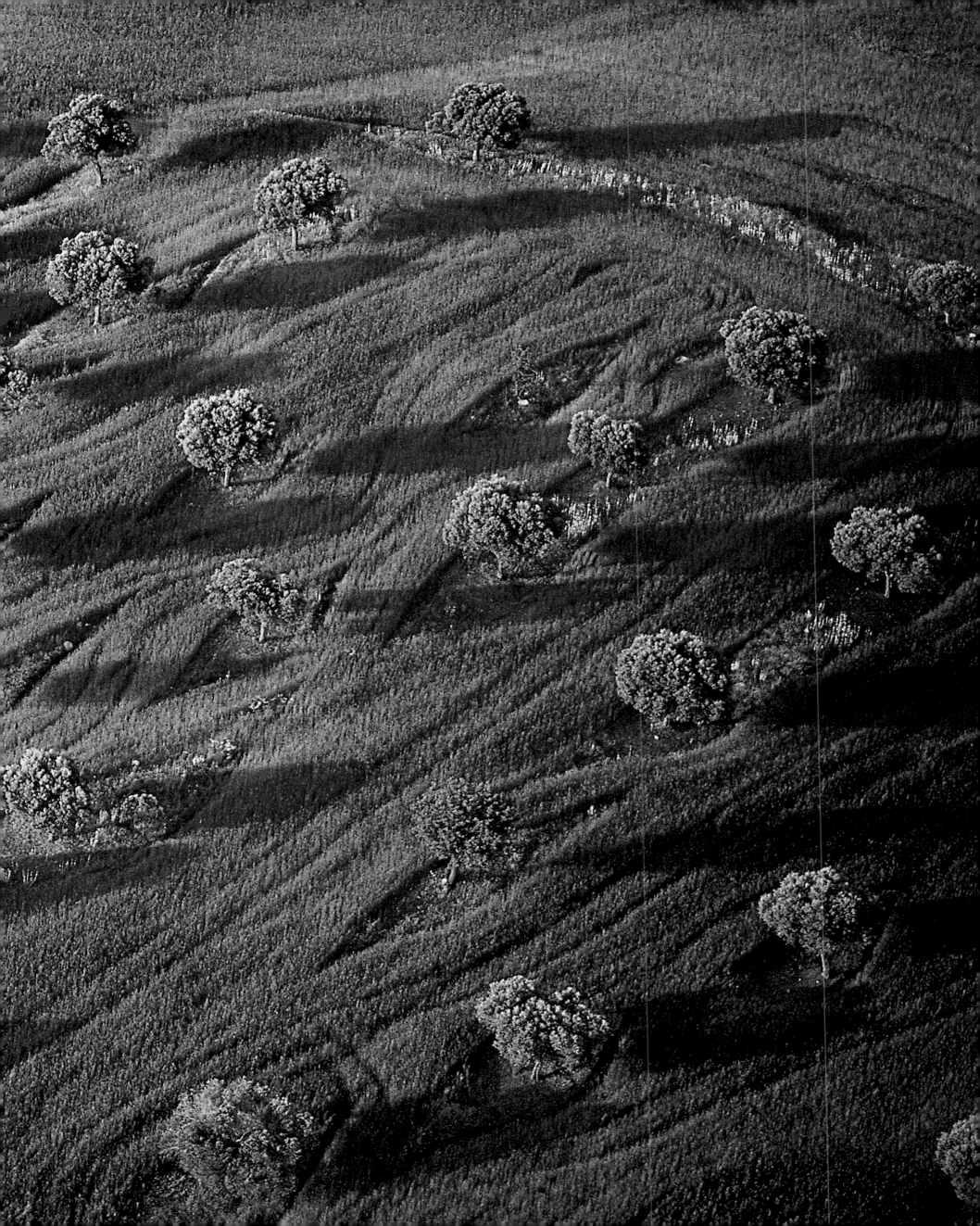

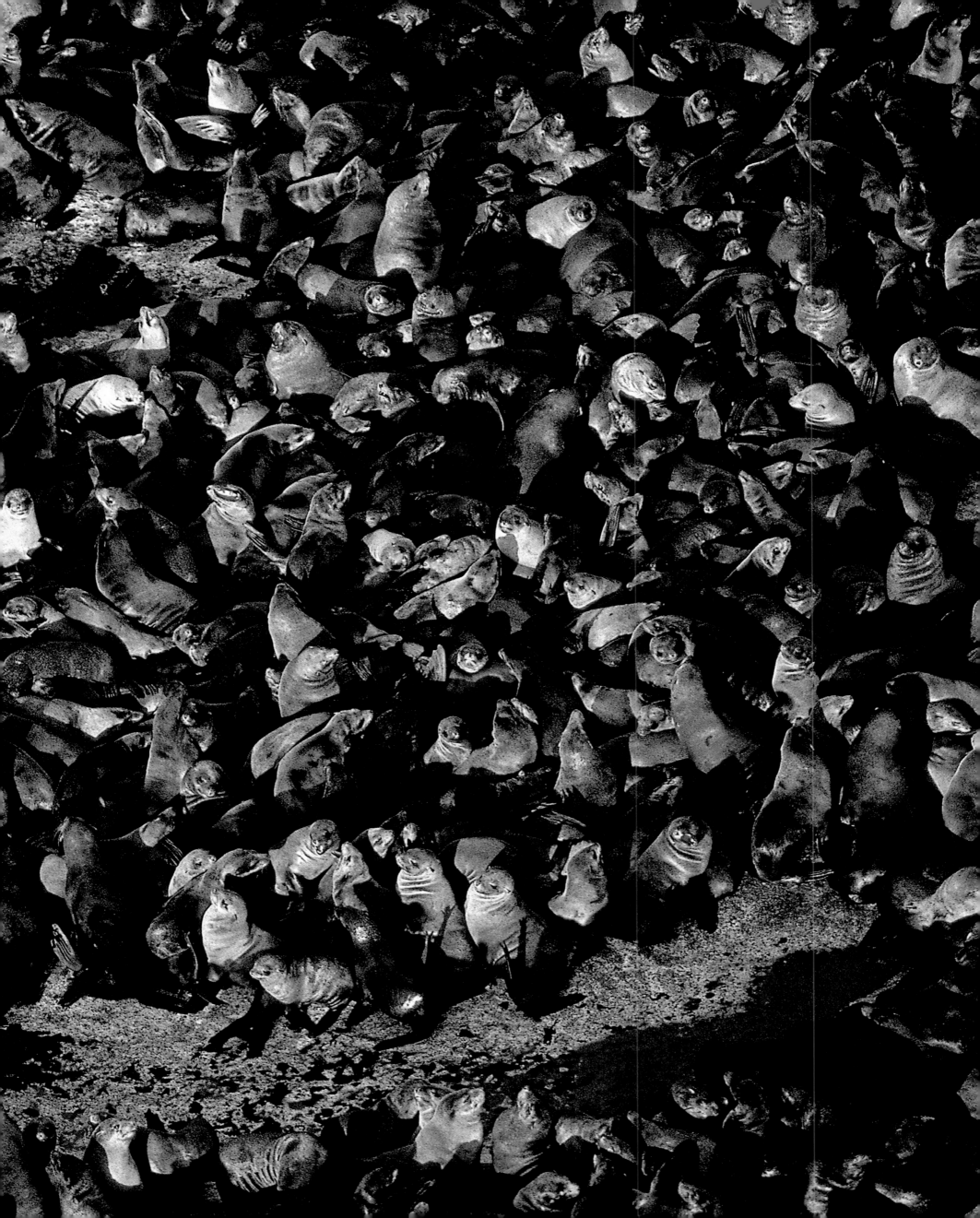

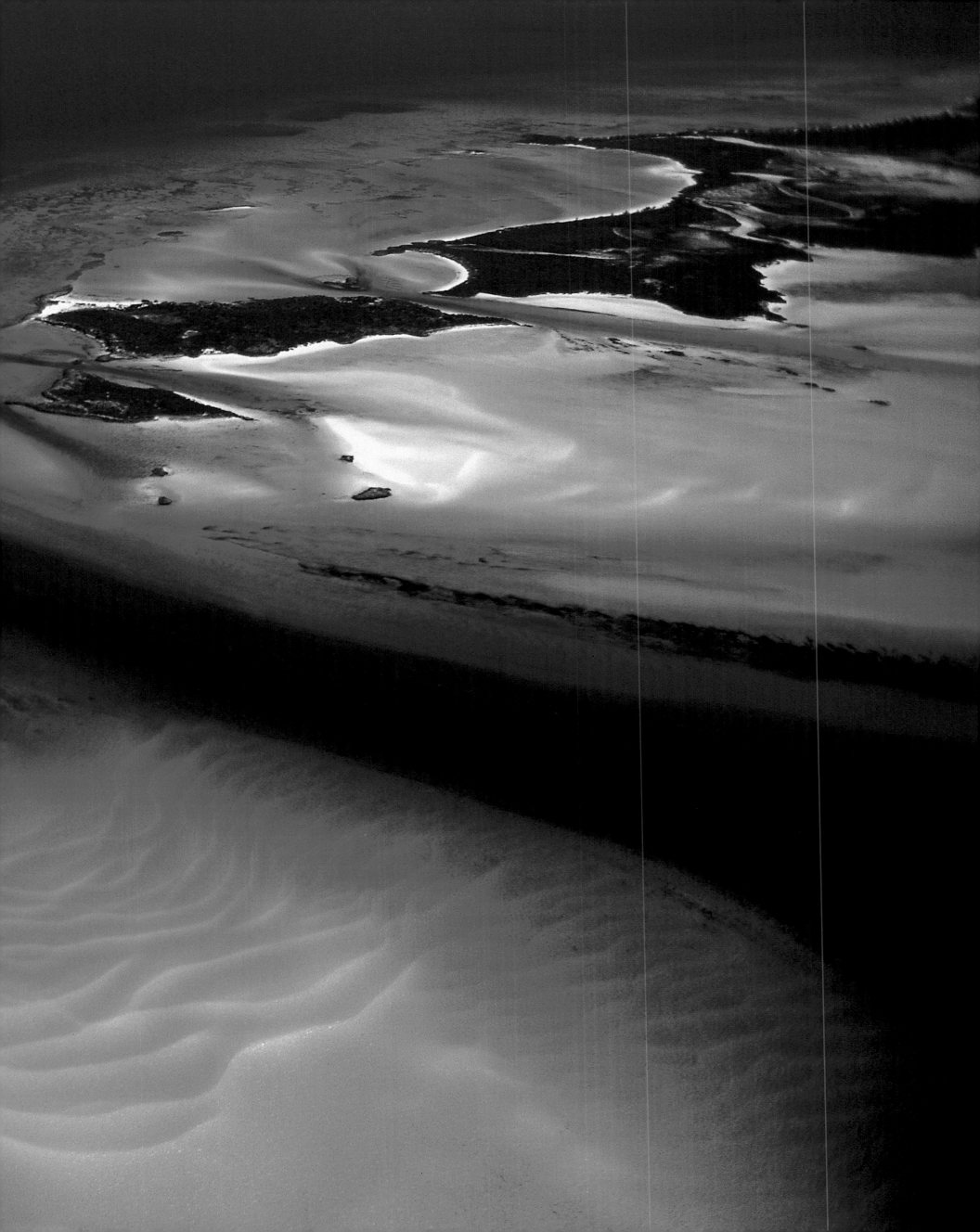

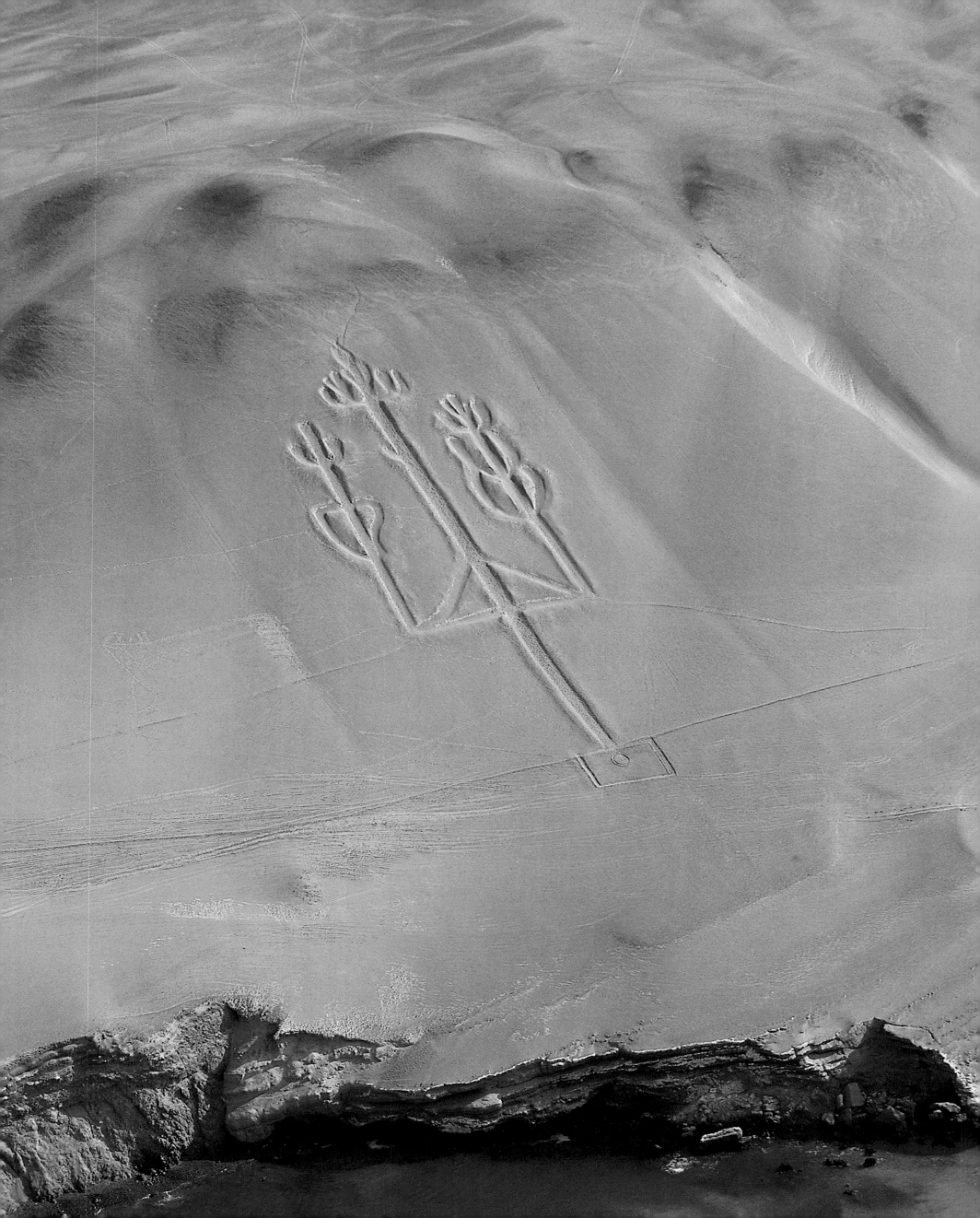

A WOUNDED ENVIRONMENT

At the turn of the twenty-first century, the collision between human activities and the biosphere, the living terrestrial world as a whole, is both global and irreversible. It affects immense populations: 4 million people were exposed to the nuclear catastrophe of Chernobyl in 1986; 20 million experience the smog of Mexico City; 60 million, in India and Bengal, are at risk from floods, a threat aggravated every year by the deforestation of the Himalayan slopes; more than 200 million could have their lives shattered by the rise in the ocean level by the end of the twenty-first century; and the depletion of the ozone layer, which protects life from excessive ultraviolet rays, concerns every one of us.

---

p. 248
CANDELABRA OF PARACAS PENINSULA, Peru
Commonly referred to as the "Candelabra," this design some 650 feet (200 m) high by 200 feet (60 m) wide is carved in the cliff of Paracas Peninsula on the Peruvian coast. Specialists believe that it depicts a cactus or the Southern Cross constellation. Although it shows some similarities with the famous designs at Nazca about 125 miles (200 km) southeast of here, it is the product of an earlier civilization, that of the Paracas. A Paraca necropolis was discovered in the region, with 429 mummified corpses, or funeral *fardos*. The Paracas, known for their textiles, embroidery, and pottery, were primarily a fishing people. Their civilization faded out about 650 B.C. The Candelabra, visible from far out at sea, was a navigational landmark, as it still is today for boats cruising off the peninsula.

FROM AGRICULTURE TO MONOCULTURE: THE END OF NATURE?

After ten millennia of development, agriculture has, in the past half-century, become a virtual mining activity. Since the end of World War II, an immense agricultural effort has quadrupled the production of grain in the world, but this success has its flip side. During the same period, the quantity of pesticides has multiplied by a factor of twenty-five, and the amount of synthetic fertilizers has grown from 14 million to more than 160 million tons. The ecological effect is severe: untimely clearings, destruction of soils, and water pollution.

We see everywhere the triumph of synthesized ecosystems, the functional units of the living world such as a forest, a lake, or a prairie. The "cultivated" forest and the "agrosystems" (cultivated ecosystems) are replacing nature. More and more high-risk monocultures exist. In all of Southeast Asia, the IR-36 variety of rice occupies two-thirds of the rice paddies. Today, twenty-nine species of plant provide more than 95 percent of human consumption all over the world, as opposed to a hundred species at the beginning of the century.

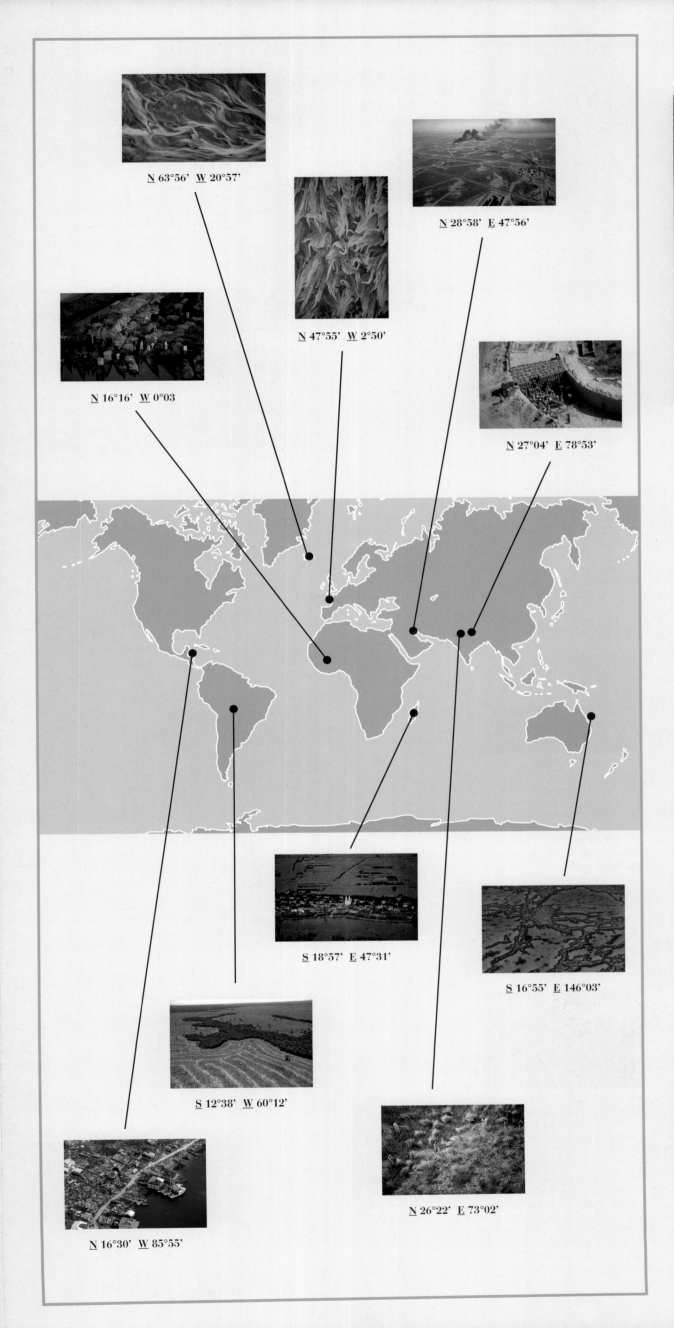

is a determining factor in the erosion of
uction of many living species. This is one
ular proofs of the planetary ecological
vas one of the major issues in the famous
d in Rio de Janeiro, Brazil, in 1992. The
rsity originates in intensive agricultural
lly in the disappearance of tropical rain
ts shelter more than 50 percent of the
species of the globe. One reason among
t the intertropical zones have been less
latitudes to the great climatic shifts that
h geological period.
he result of more than 3.6 billion years
ters the future evolutions of life, but it is
l toward extinction. The earth has already
eriods of ecological upheaval that set off
tinction. Today we are in the sixth great
Evidence suggests that the dual effect of
e industrialization of agriculture plays a
mean that humanity alone is responsible.

ND SOILS IN DANGER

n essential resource for agriculture. Agri-
for three-fourths of its consumption glob-
veloping countries, for nearly all of it (92

percent in China, 90 percent in India a
tion is already encountering serious s
regions of the world: northeastern Afric
sula; northern China; the plains of the In
Great Plains in the United States, where
gation now depends on the water of th
Irrigation systems often suffer from lack
ous regions are affected by the salinatio
percent of irrigated lands), Pakistan (
America (40 percent), and North Ameri

    The ecological costs of agriculture a
the size of interferences in the biogeoch
cially those of nitrogen and phosphorus
by runoff waters or drained toward grou
sible for massive pollution in all regions
to intensive systems of agriculture and l

    Long considered as a receptacle for
nite dilutive capacities and as an inexhaus
resources, the world's oceans are also s
Coastal zones such as estuaries and con
among the ecologically richest and most
the outlets of polluted rivers, these zone
degraded. The accelerated extinction of

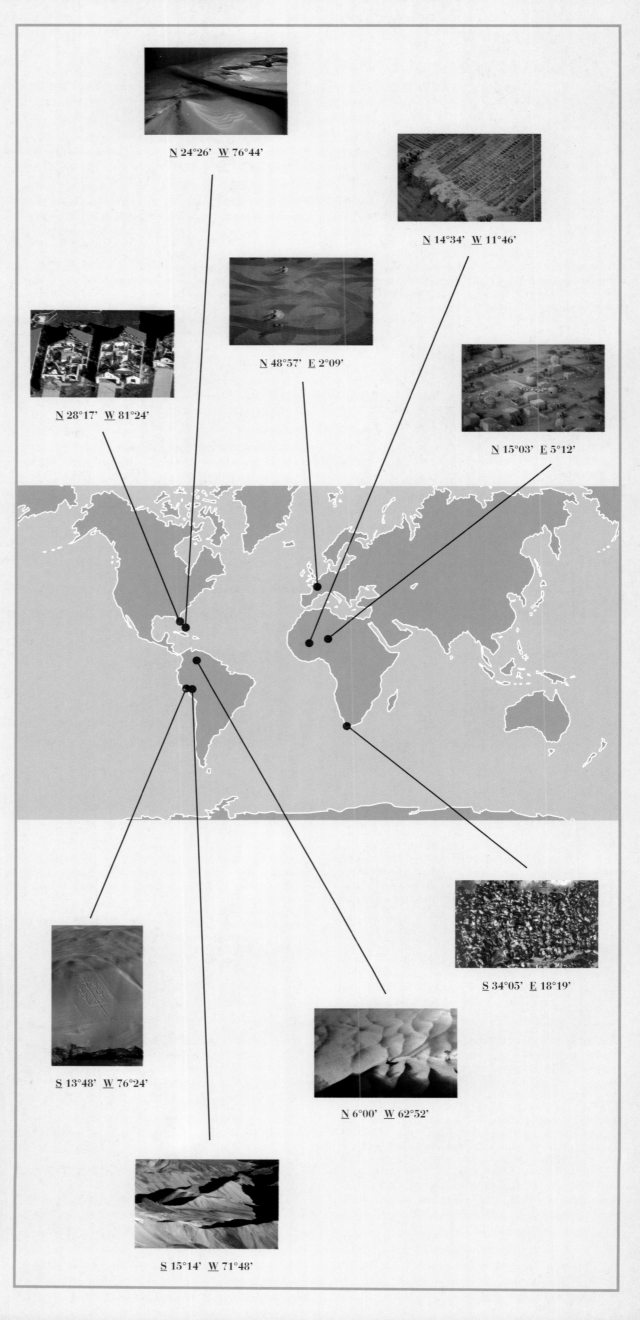

<u>N</u> 24°26' <u>W</u> 76°44'

<u>N</u> 14°34' <u>W</u> 11°46'

<u>N</u> 48°57' <u>E</u> 2°09'

<u>N</u> 28°17' <u>W</u> 81°24'

<u>N</u> 15°03' <u>E</u> 5°12'

<u>S</u> 34°05' <u>E</u> 18°19'

<u>S</u> 13°48' <u>W</u> 76°24'

<u>N</u> 6°00' <u>W</u> 62°52'

<u>S</u> 15°14' <u>W</u> 71°48'

THE NEW VOLCANISM AND
URBAN INDUSTRY

The most spectacular changes, however, have been caused by the growth of heavy industries (chemistry, metallurgy, and energy, for example). Poorly controlled technological innovation or criminal negligence accompanies the quest for profit "at any price." This can lead to tragic consequences: in the 1950s in Minamata, Japan, mercury used by the paper industry killed several hundred people; dioxin pollution caused tremendous harm in Italy in 1976; the wreckage of the *Amoco Cadiz* in France in 1978 and the sinking of the *Exxon Valdez* off the coast of Alaska in 1989 created enormous oil spills and immense ecological damage. The dissemination of products such as DDT and other pesticides, explosive agents, asbestos, and radioactive elements are also causing the deterioration of the environment.

Pollution of the atmosphere has reached disastrous proportions. After World War II the industrial system created an artificial volcanism. Atmospheric pollution in the last twenty years of the twentieth century has become an enormous problem in emerging industrial nations such as China, where heavy industry relies primarily on coal. Several kinds of pollutants are having a growing effect on the biosphere, including the colossal quantities of air emissions from the combustion of various forms of fossil fuel: carbonic gas, which is not a direct health threat but causes global warming; carbon monoxide; unburned hydrocarbons; nitrous oxides; sulfur dioxide and trioxide, the source of acid rains that affect many forests, especially in Europe and North America. The effect of atmospheric micropollutants and diverse particles in the form of aerosols is no less harmful. And the radioactive fallout of nuclear accidents has particularly dramatic consequences. With the Chernobyl catastrophe of April 26, 1986, human history entered a new phase.

The growth of automobile traffic is a factor in specifically urban forms of air pollution. Despite the continuous improvement in engines, the growing number of cars in circulation and the increase in highways are making "automobile civilization" more and more dangerous to human health. If all of humanity attained the level of automobile use that exists in the United States, the total number of automobiles in the world would rise from 500 million to 3 billion. This is an intolerable scenario, considering its environmental effects. The start of the twenty-first century could mark the ephemeral apogee of an automobile civilization soon asphyxiated by its own success.

The question is now raised: after hundreds of thousands of years of evolution, are our societies now endangering the very conditions for life on earth?

Jean-Paul Deléage

---

p. 257
ALGAE IN THE GULF OF MORBIHAN, France
An epidemic in the 1920s decimated *Crassostrea angulata*, the most widely exploited oyster species in France. A Japanese species, *Crassostrea gigas*, was introduced and, involuntarily along with it, some thirty species of animals and algae that live today in the waters of the English Channel and the Atlantic Ocean. One example is the Sargasso (*Sargassum miticum*), which replaced local species here in the Gulf of Morbihan. It was feared that there might be a galloping proliferation, but this species, while becoming abundant, seems to have found its place in the ecosystem. The algae is nevertheless being carefully watched. Brittany has a sea coast of 1,700 miles (2,730 km), 70 percent of which is undergoing urbanization. It is the site of the Coastal Conservatory, which covers approximately 10,000 acres (4,000 hectares), more than half of which contains sites with an area of more than 250 acres (100 hectares).

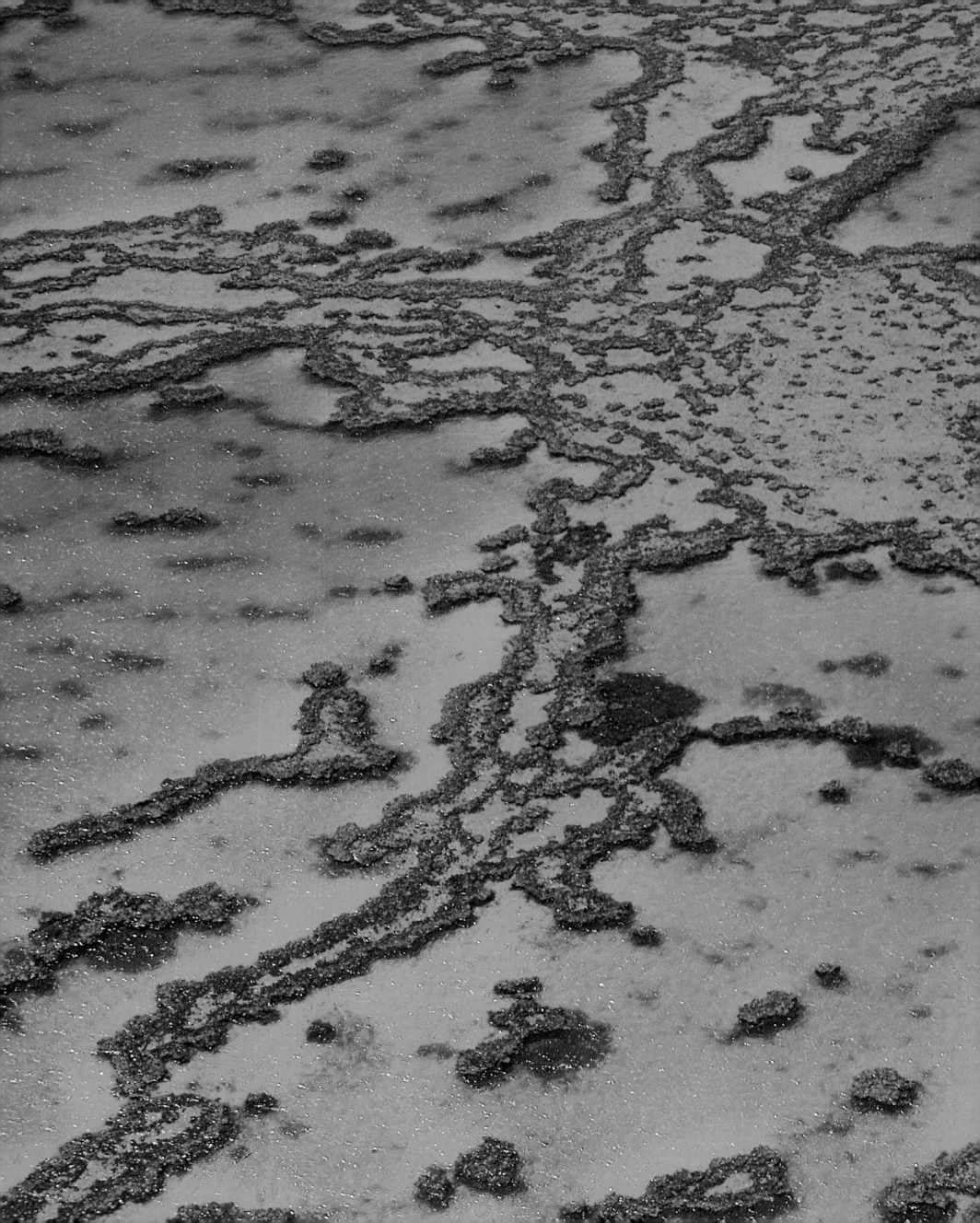

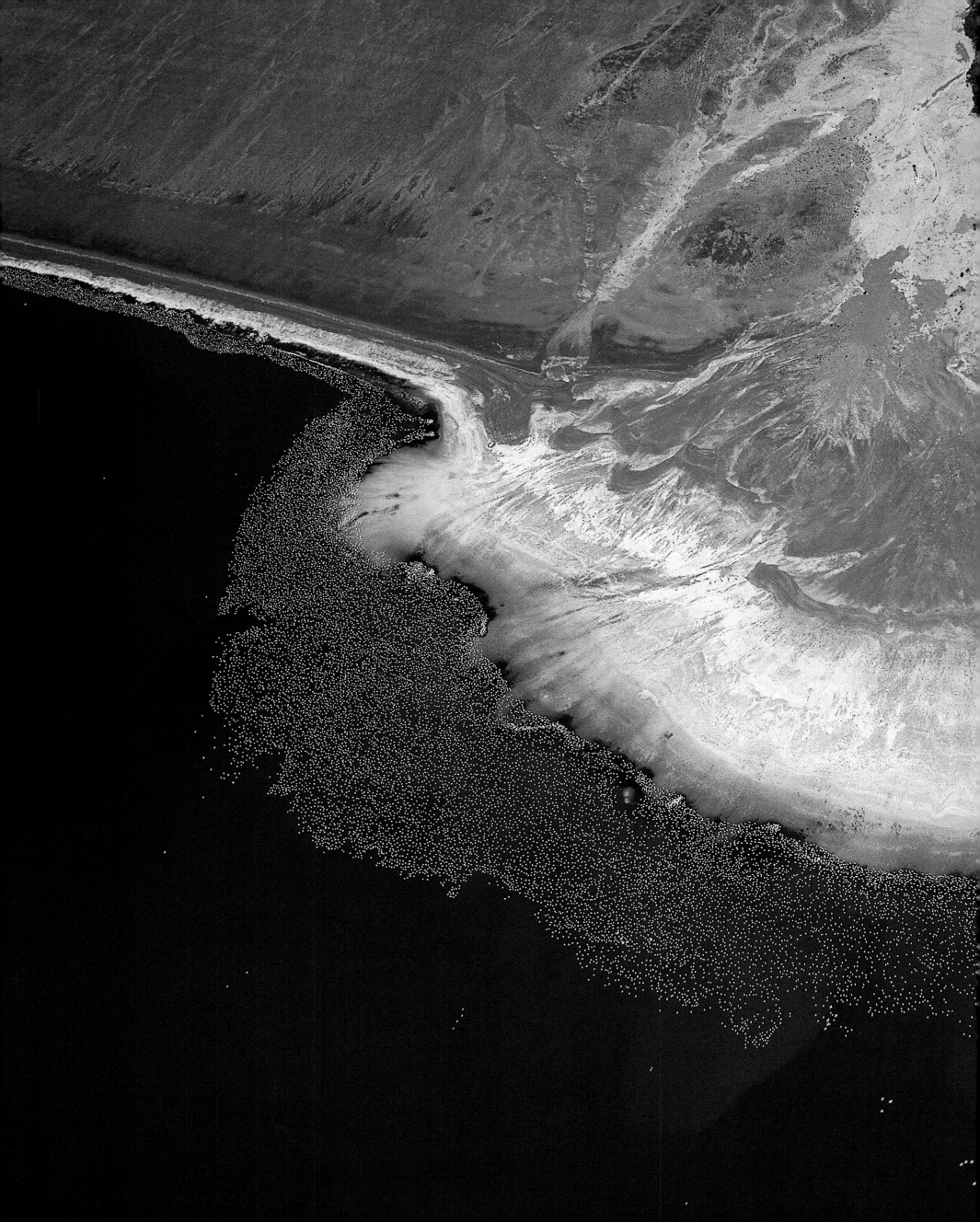

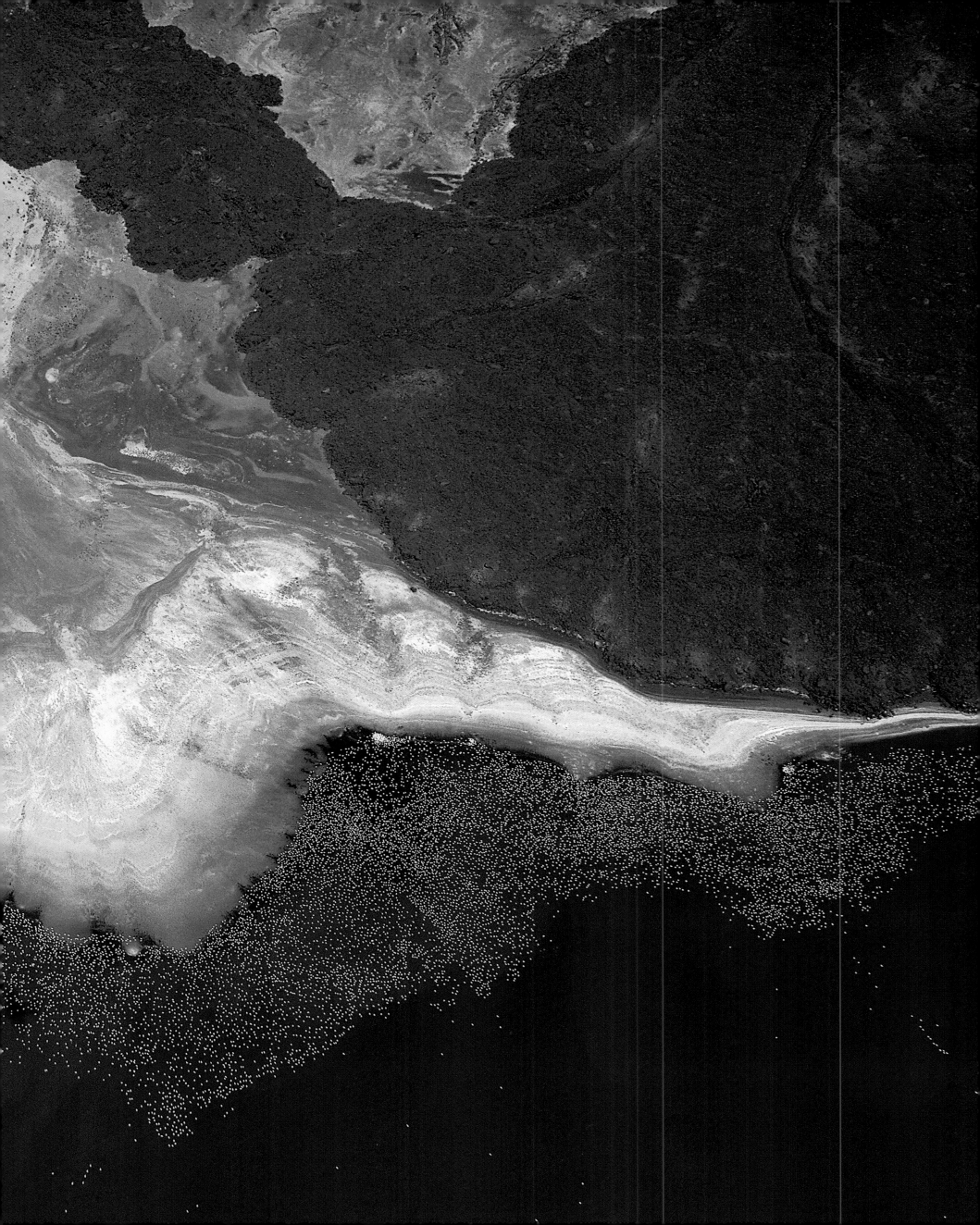

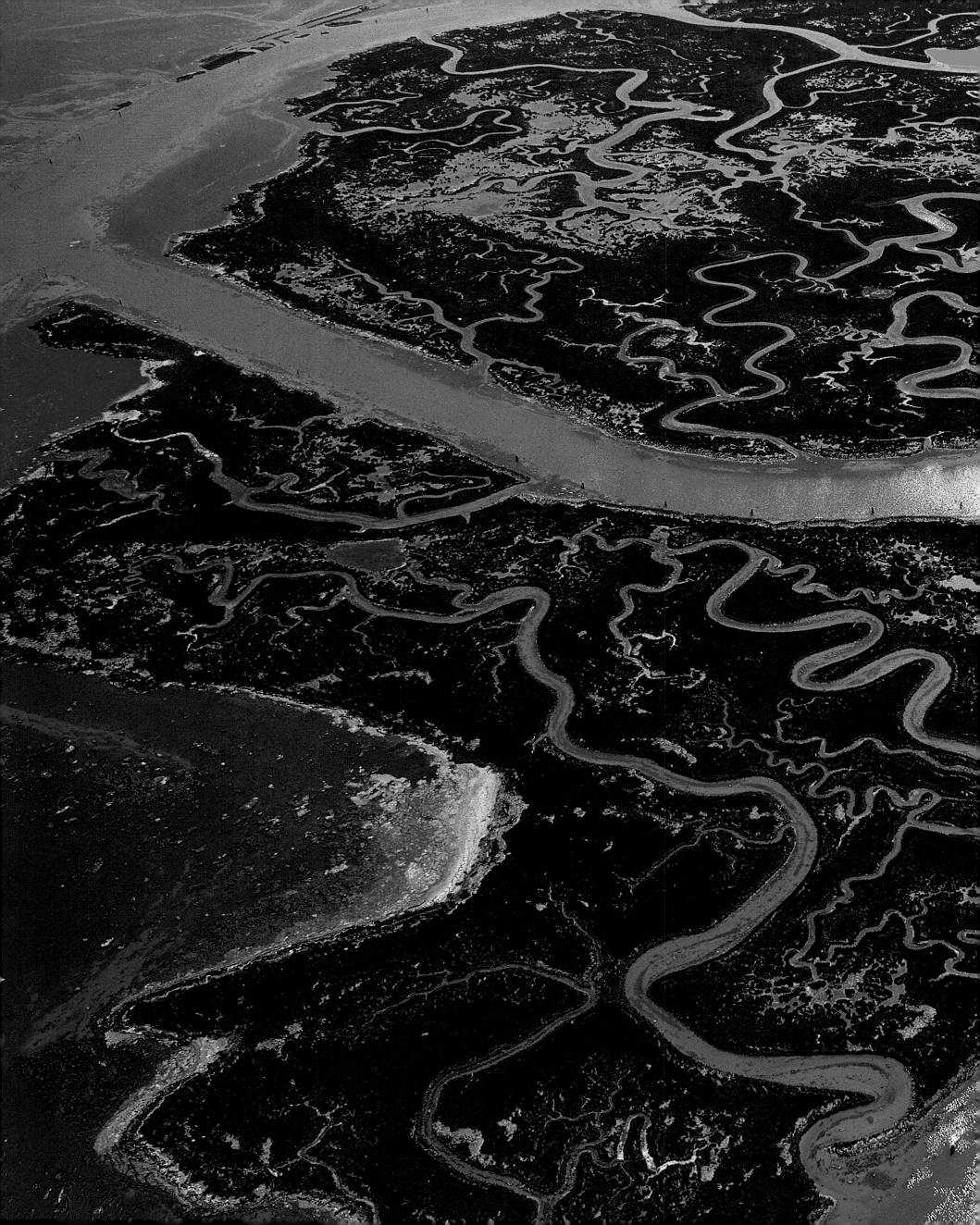

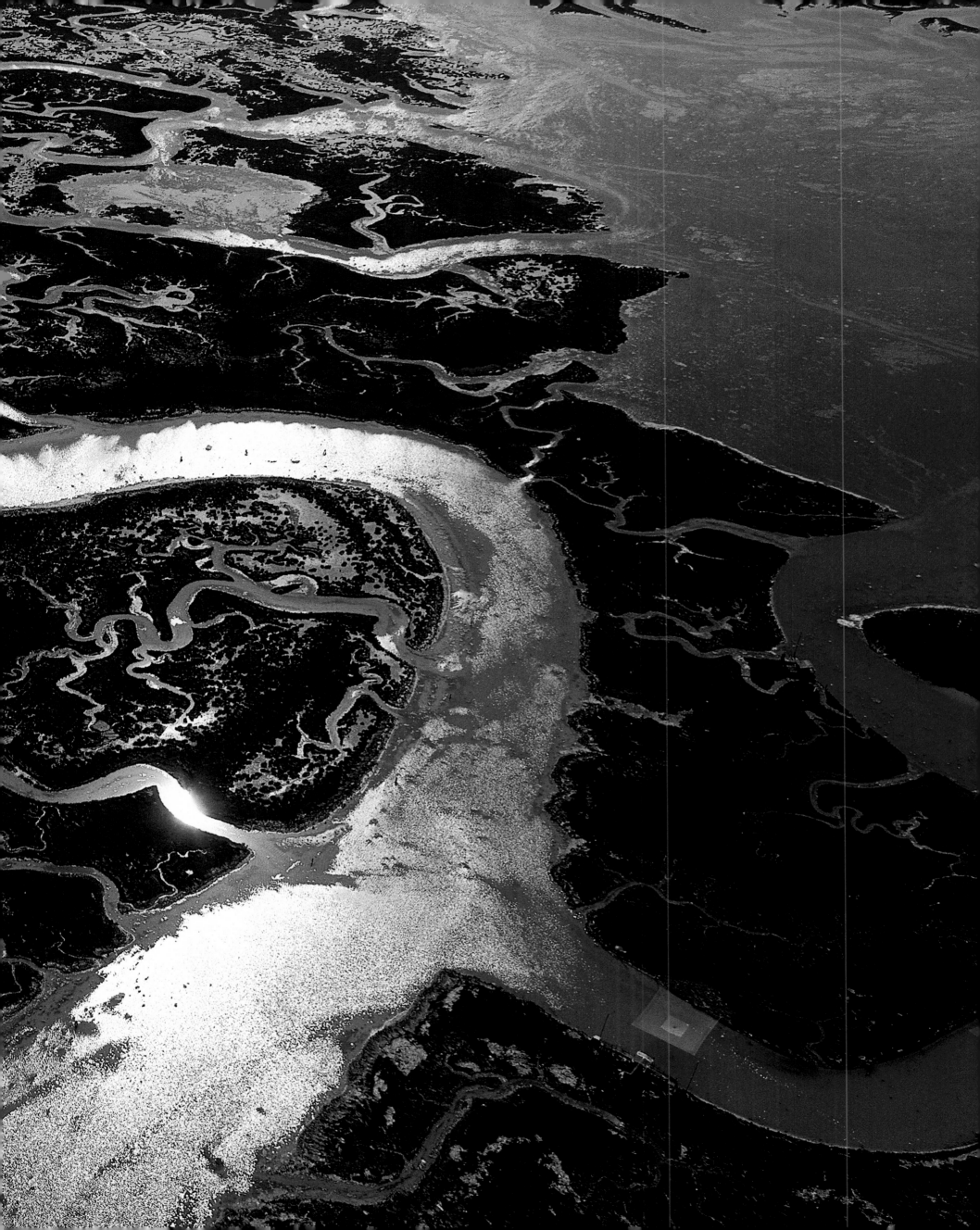

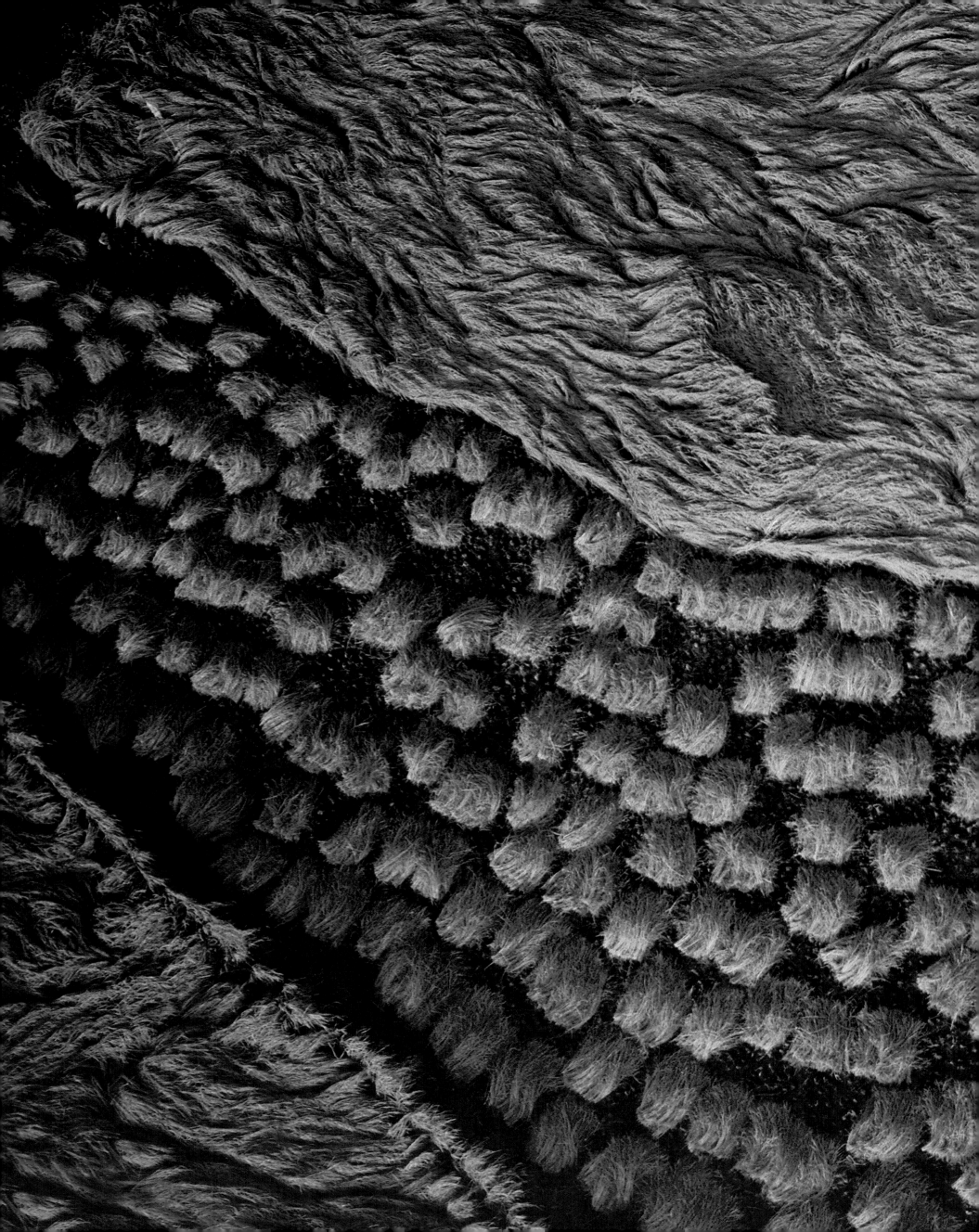

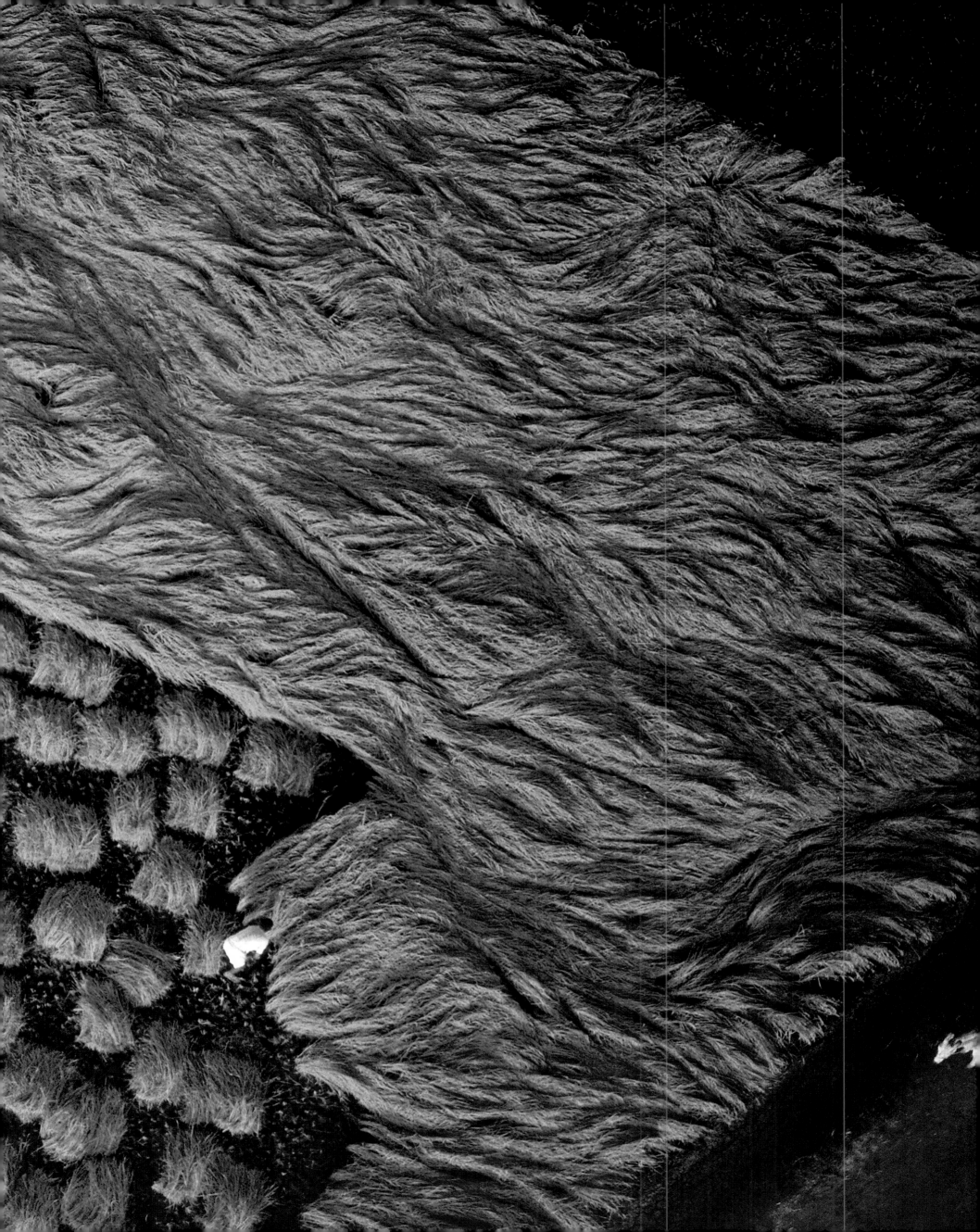

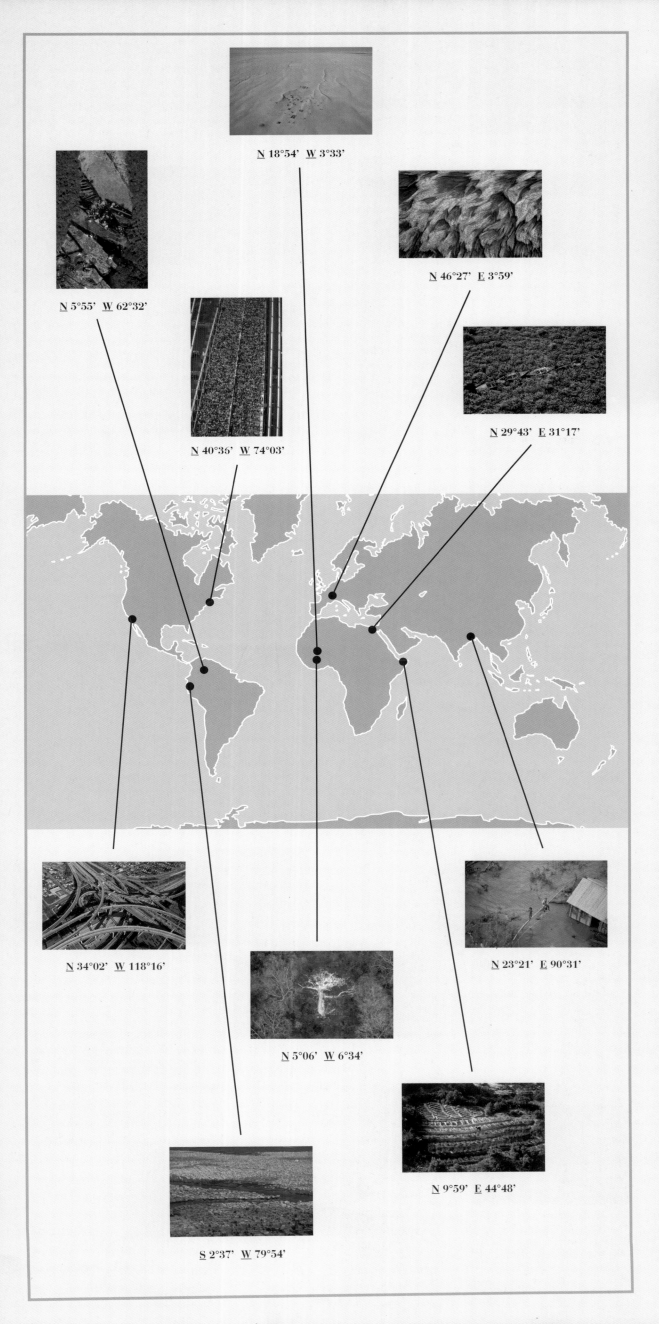

N 18°54' W 3°33'

N 5°55' W 62°32'

N 46°27' E 3°59'

N 40°36' W 74°03'

N 29°43' E 31°17'

N 34°02' W 118°16'

N 5°06' W 6°34'

N 23°21' E 90°31'

N 9°59' E 44°48'

S 2°37' W 79°54'

deny that the challenges faced by the
d in the future are in part due to popu-
hould we hold that increase solely respon-
nt development of the poorest nations
y of environmental damage. Population
al factors in a complex equation; con-
of technology are two others. For exam-
t enough potable drinking water, we can
opulation as a source of the problem: as
bitants increases, so does the consump-
dustrial and agricultural waste and pol-
rivers are equally important issues.
st not be an obstacle to raising the stan-
cularly among the poorest. The future of
ends largely on our capacity to reconcile
nd healthy, lasting development.

LIZATION SCENARIO

ple will inhabit the world of the future?
regularly undertakes the delicate task of
population long term. Stabilization is a
scenario. Some years ago it was thought
ulation would stabilize at 12 billion in
population would have to double one last

time to attain a steady state in which the b
tries would guarantee renewal of generatio
estimations put that stabilization figure at
ference is explained by an unexpectedly
birthrate, particularly in China. If this sce
stabilization is realized, two major transfo
a very significant aging of the population w
matic shift in the distribution of the earth

At present almost a third of the w
younger than fifteen years old. With a p
tion under conditions we can reasonably e
population in 150 years' time would be ov
As the French demographer Alfred Sauvy
of "grow or grow old." It is difficult to

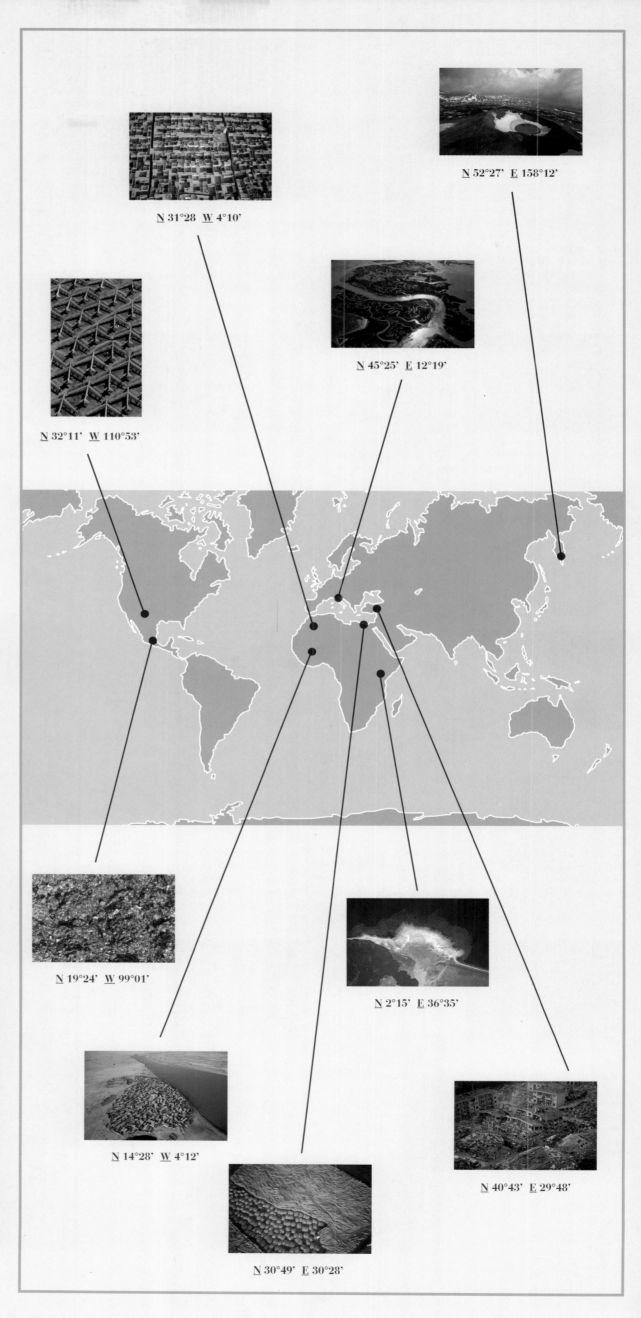

N 31°28' W 4°10'

N 52°27' E 158°12'

N 32°11' W 110°53'

N 45°25' E 12°19'

N 19°24' W 99°01'

N 2°15' E 36°35'

N 14°28' W 4°12'

N 30°49' E 30°28'

N 40°43' E 29°48'

past, but one of the most progressive advances in human history has been the successful combat against early mortality—at the price of a population spurt. One assumption is that the widespread use of contraceptives will ensure a population balance, but this is not an entirely accepted prediction.

However, it is missing the point to make population stabilization a precondition for economic development. In order to achieve global population stability, minimal development is needed to persuade countries in the Southern Hemisphere to adopt new patterns of behavior or pursue social changes. Feeding the hungry, unemployment, and public health are among the issues that we must deal with now. The 6 billion people who are alive today and the 8 or 9 billion of tomorrow must be able to feed themselves but also to live without overburdening the environment and without doing it irreparable harm. One of the great challenges facing the human race is to redress the inequalities between the Northern and Southern Hemispheres while making sure that newly developing countries do not make the same environmental mistakes as today's richest nations.

Striking inequality is not only found between hemispheres, however; extreme poverty can exist alongside extreme wealth even within the same country. For example, the inequalities between men and women are pronounced in many areas. Women are sometimes at a disadvantage because they live in a poor region or one that is in crisis, such as the Sahel or Haiti. But other causes are culturally ingrained: the great inequality in education between men and women, as in southern Asia; the strong preference for male offspring, as

in China; the practice of genital mutilation of female children, as in West and East Africa and the Middle East; the very early age for marriage, as in sub-Saharan Africa; and spousal violence in areas throughout the world.

At the world conferences held at the initiative of the United Nations during the 1990s and the 1995 conference in Beijing, delegates stated the necessity of improving the status of women. This is a matter of vital importance for development and a necessary condition for the stabilization of the world population. For the birthrate to continue to decline, the status of women must rise.

Population stabilization is not the solution to the problems we face today. It is necessary, but it is an impossible first step. Developing nations must create environmentally sound models of economic development and address the immediate issues of inequality and poverty.

Jacques Véron

---

p. 297
RIVER ON THE AUYAN TEPUÍ, Gran Sabana region, Venezuela
The Gran Sabana region in southeastern Venezuela is a wide plain covered with savannas and dense forest, interrupted by imposing mesas of sandy rock, known as *tepuís*. The mesa of Auyan Tepuí, or "devil's mountain," covers 275 square miles (700 km²) and rises to 8,500 feet (2,580 m). The Rio Carrao zigzags across Auyan Tepuí and, at its edge, plunges in a steep waterfall. The Salto del Angel waterfall is the world's highest free-falling waterway; at a height of 3,210 feet (979 m), it is fifteen times higher than Niagara Falls. Rich in gold and diamond ore, the Gran Sabana region and its many waterways have attracted prospectors since 1930. They have been especially drawn to towns like Icabaru, which was made famous by the discovery of a diamond of more than 150 carats, called El Dorado, a name that conjures up the days of the conquistadors.

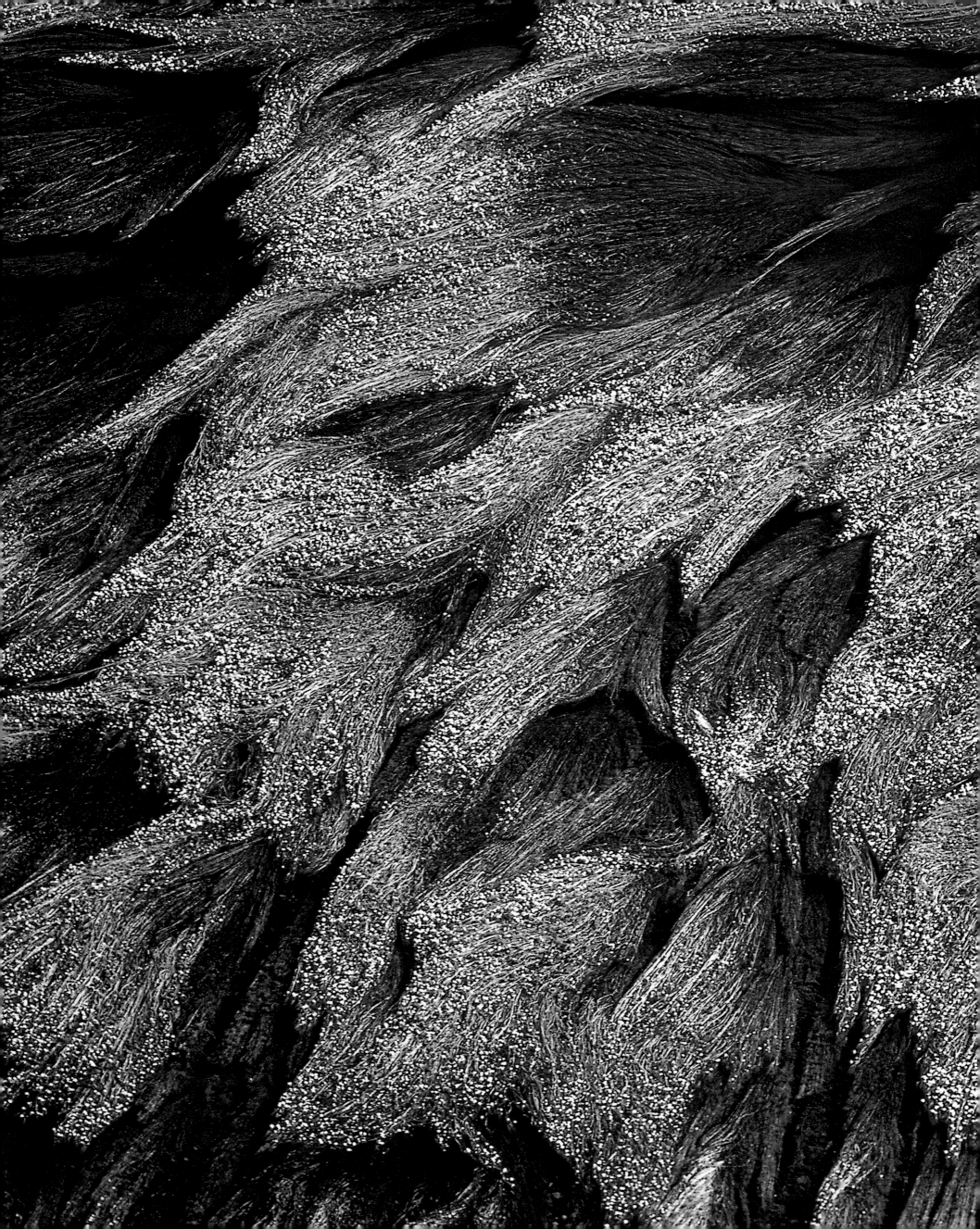

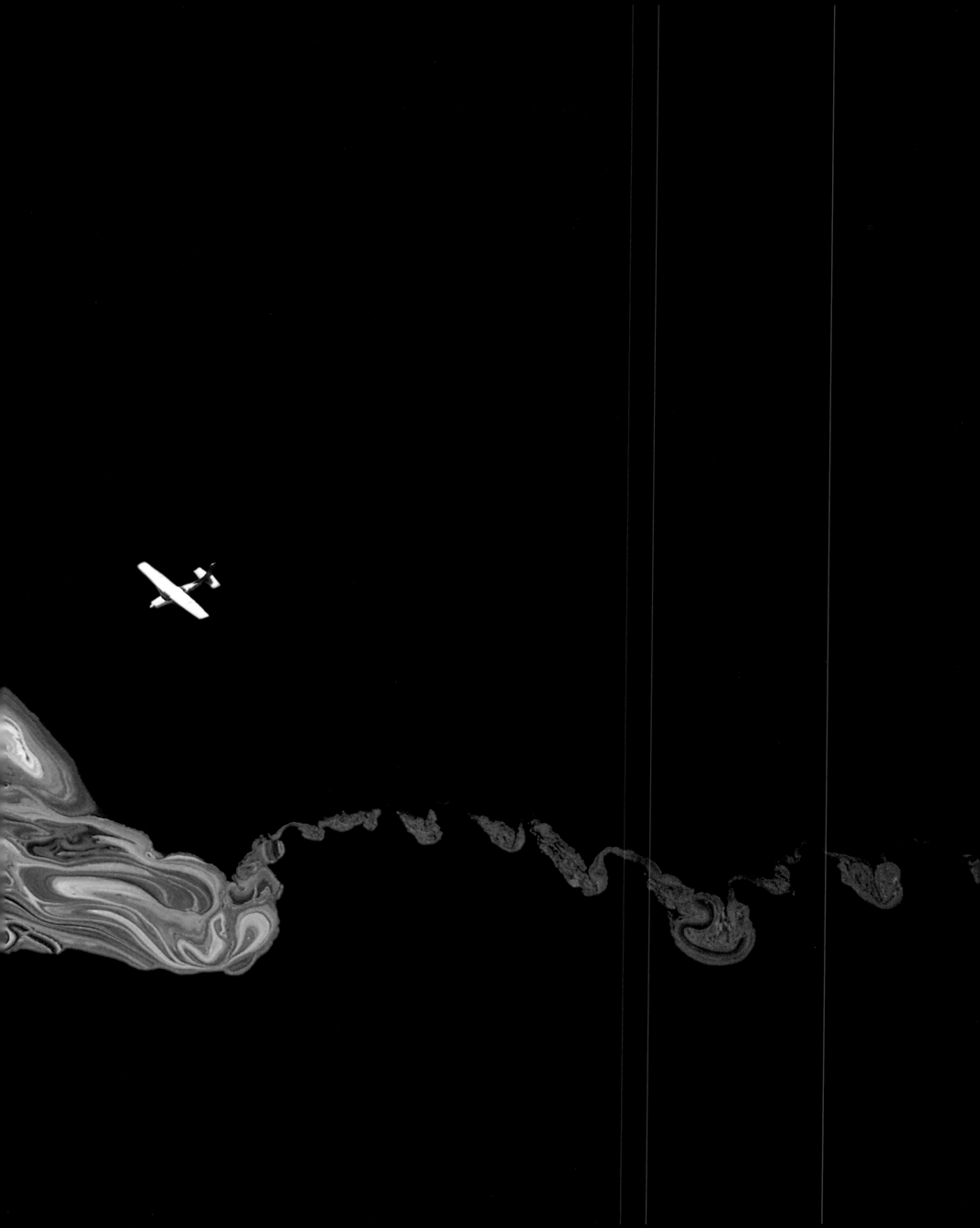

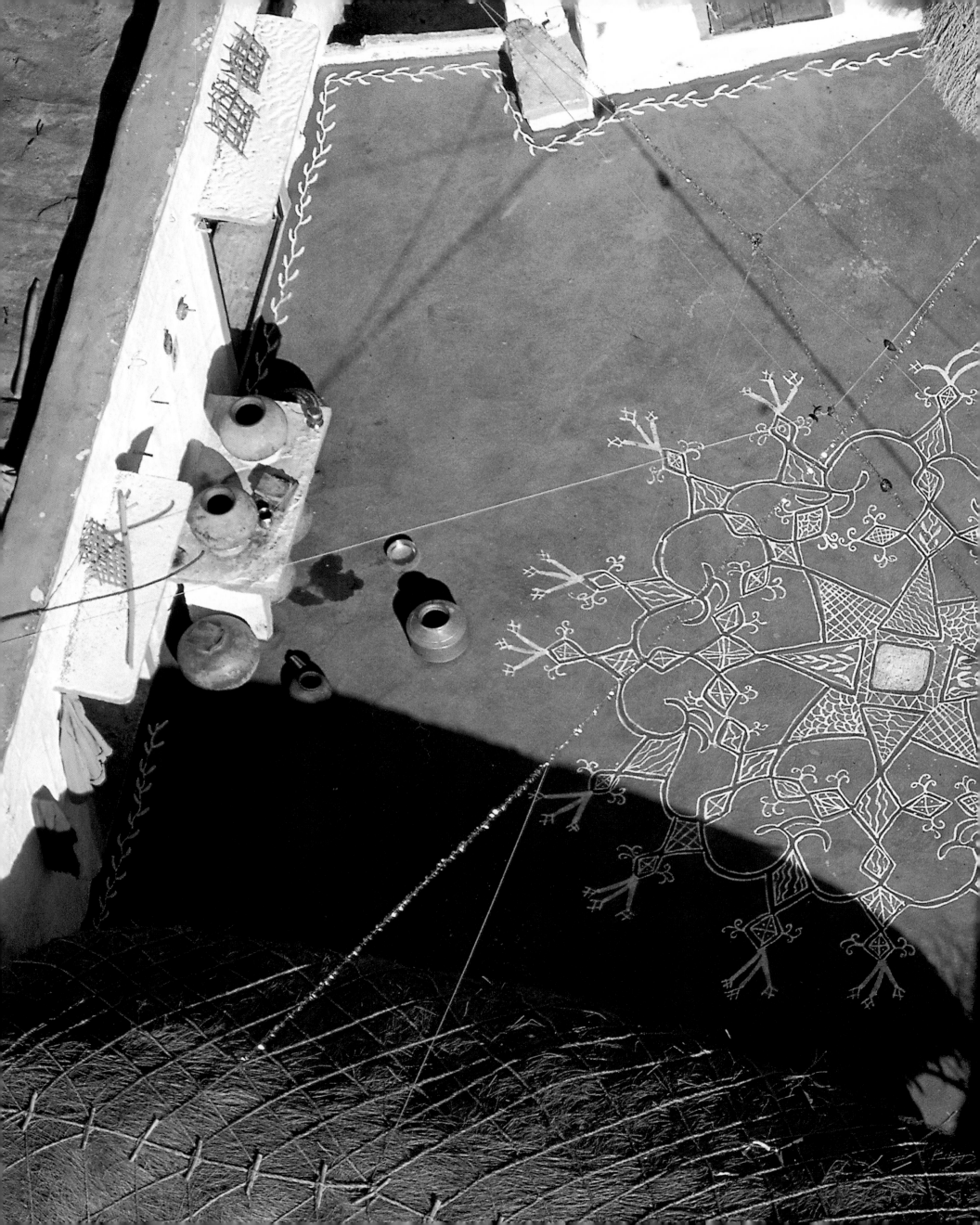

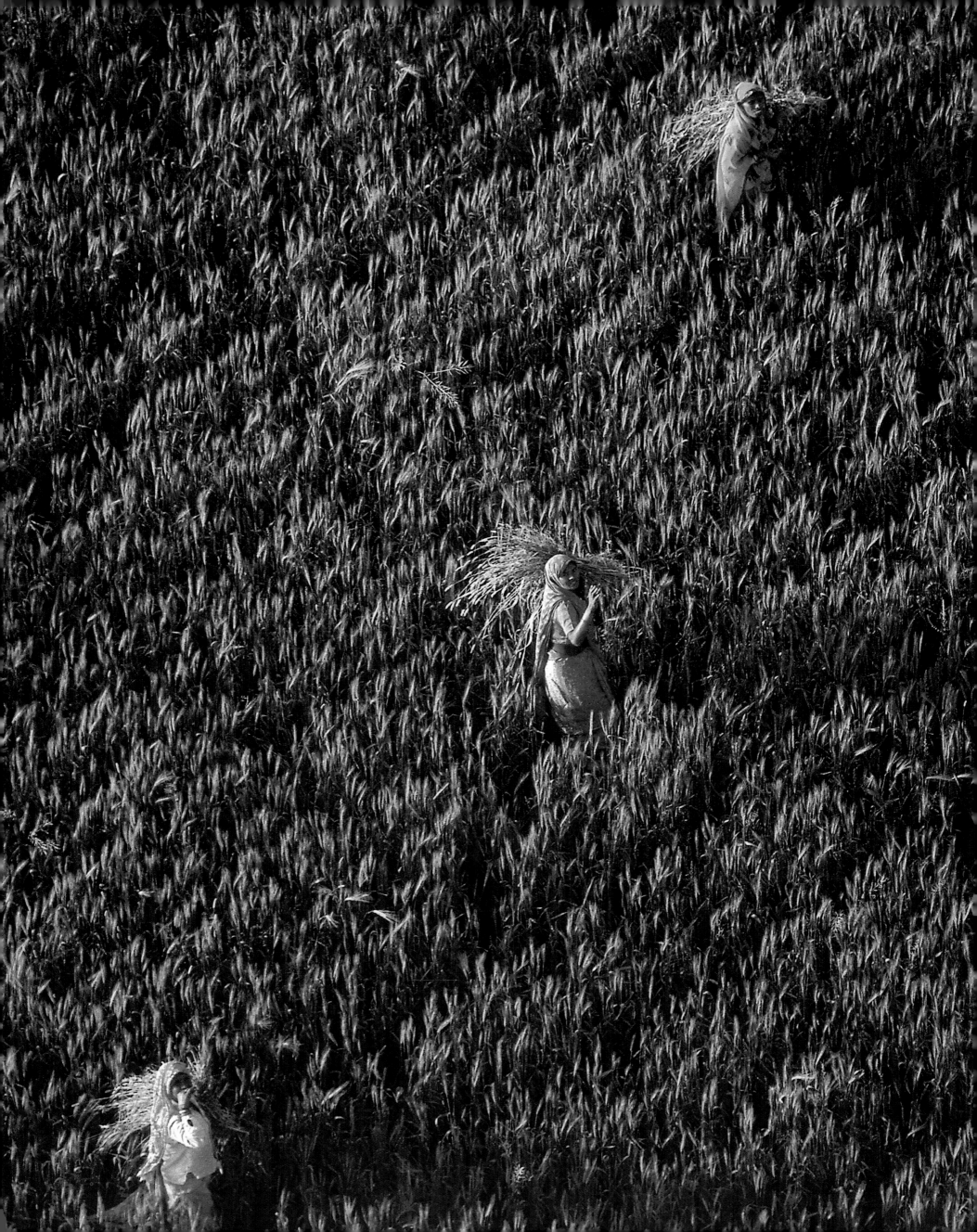

GROWING ENOUGH TO FEED
THE WORLD

Is our planet unable to meet increasing demands caused by the mathematical progression of the world's population? Do we run the risk of entering a new era of global famine? In the 1960s and 1970s we were able to avert such a danger by making innovative technology available to countries with severe malnutrition. Now known as the "green revolution," the plan was meant to satisfy these countries' expanding needs and allow them to reach self-sufficiency. The results were not long in coming. Since the 1960s the growth of agricultural production worldwide has regularly outpaced the growth of population, even in the most heavily populated countries of the Southern Hemisphere. Large countries formerly plagued by recurrent famine experienced a boom: in a span of twenty years, grain production in India more than tripled and in China increased by more than 50 percent, while pork production in both countries quadrupled. Progress was so striking that today we should, in theory, be able to feed the entire population of the globe. Famines have disappeared, except in countries at war or where leaders use food as a political weapon.

According to some predictions, however, famine could return in the coming century. A new era of food insecurity could result from a war unleashed by an overflowing population in a world with limited riches. Overexploitation of nonrenewable natural resources, the predatory nature of modern agriculture, and accelerating urbanization that each year appropriates millions of acres of arable land have all contributed to slowing down the growth of food production at the very moment that the earth is experiencing an unprecedented population explosion.

A CATASTROPHIC PROJECTION

The increase in the starvation rate has not matched the population increase, but for some 800 million people in the southern hemisphere—almost 200 million in Africa and more than 500 million in Asia—starvation continues. Available statistics confirm the worst fears: according to the United Nations Food and Agriculture Organization (FAO), the population of non-freshwater fish has had a zero increase between 1990 and 1996, grain production worldwide has only increased by 0.5 percent per year since the beginning of the 1990s, and per capita grain supply declined by 1.1 percent.

Several researchers have nonetheless strongly challenged this gloomy picture. If it is true that between 1950 and 1980 the population has grown at an alarming rate, in the past ten years the *rate* of growth has dramatically slowed down. In addition, food production worldwide has up to now largely met the challenge of demographic growth, and the theoretical per capita grain supply has risen in the past fifty years. The FAO, which now posits 1,900 calories a day as the min-

---

p. 328

WHEAT HARVEST IN THE REGION OF MATHURA, Uttar Pradesh, India
The state of Uttar Pradesh is located in the country's most fertile region, blessed with alluvial terrain that is permanently irrigated by the waters of the Ganges and its many tributaries fed by the Himalayan snows. The climate of this state, which is marked by mild winters and hot, humid summers, also contributes to making it one of the greatest agricultural regions of the country. Wheat, a major local crop, as shown here near Mathura, is harvested manually by women at the end of the dry season; it is raised mostly for local consumption and for the national market. With an annual harvest of 69 million tons, India is among the world's leading wheat producers, ranked just behind China and equal to the United States.

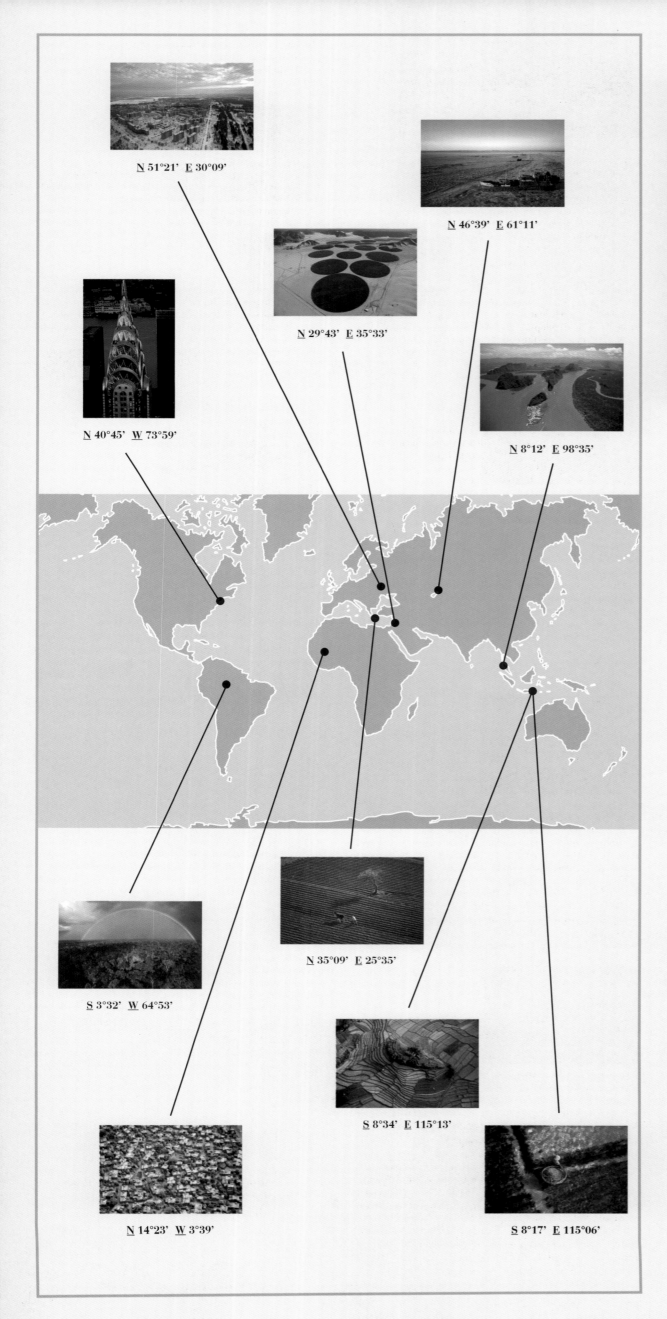

N 51°21' E 30°09'

N 46°39' E 61°11'

N 29°43' E 35°33'

N 40°45' W 73°59'

N 8°12' E 98°35'

S 3°32' W 64°53'

N 35°09' E 25°35'

S 8°34' E 115°13'

N 14°23' W 3°39'

S 8°17' E 115°06'

...forecasts conceal important regional dis-
...n-belt Asia, which has a predominantly
...ountries such as Bangladesh are facing
...ems. The situation of sub-Saharan Africa,
...0 percent of the population is still largely
...disturbing; this region may replace Asia
...e highest rate of malnutrition. The FAO
...the number of Africans suffering from
...se by 70 percent in fifteen years, rising
...1990 to 296 million by 2010, when the
...Asia will be at 200 million.

...IES AND
...ION MODELS

...owever, is not the only factor to be con-
...o reveal that the number of undernour-
...ecline over the next fifteen years—regard-
...production increases—unless specific
...are enacted. It is scandalous that hunger
...planet that produces everything in abun-
...ecause of the uneven distribution of this
...lobe.
...ronic hunger remains restricted to the
...d to those with an extremely unequal dis-
...s, it has been easy to cite insufficient pro-

duction or climatic disturbances as the s
nutrition. Today, however, food shortage a
tion of the population of the world's leadi
ducing countries. Brazil offers almost a
world's third-largest agricultural exporte
age to feed its 160 million inhabitants ad
archaic agrarian structures inherited from
the great landholders retain disproportio
These factors help explain why 8 million
workers without land are prevented fro
alongside large landed estates that have g
guarded by private armies. More parado
rampant in the heart of the world's riches
in the United States and Western Europ

The appearance in rich countries
believed to have been eradicated will fo
sider the matter in political terms rath
technical thinking that has prevailed for
today prevents Europeans or North Ame
themselves adequately, this does not mea
of the Northern Hemisphere have globally
of food consumption. These countries, w
21 percent of the earth's population, ab

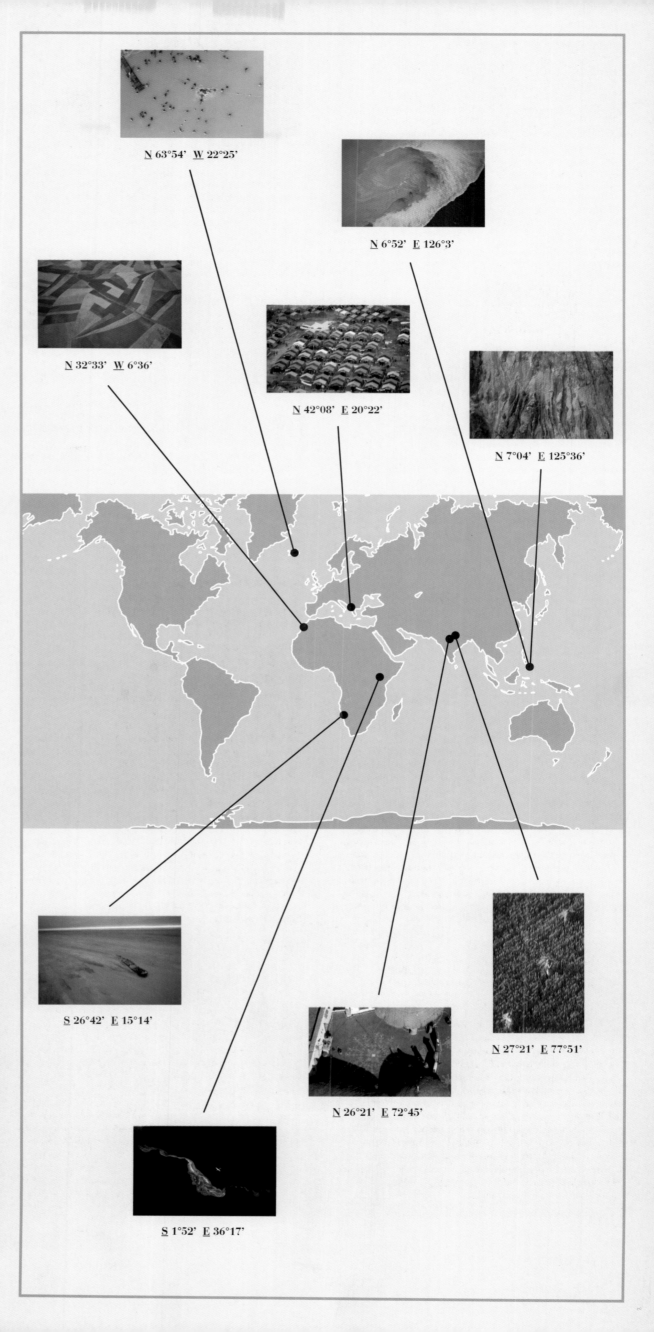

N 63°54' W 22°25'

N 6°52' E 126°3'

N 32°33' W 6°36'

N 42°08' E 20°22'

N 7°04' E 125°36'

S 26°42' E 15°14'

N 26°21' E 72°45'

N 27°21' E 77°51'

S 1°52' E 36°17'

cient enclaves of the Southern Hemisphere are causing irreversible harm to the environment. The planners of the agrarian and nutrition policies of the large producing countries show no concern about sterility of overirrigated lands in Asian regions long since devoted to the green revolution. Nor have they worried about pollution and exhaustion of the groundwater in areas where the use of chemical fertilizers has reached record heights, or about the infertility of overused soils in Europe and North America, among other alarms. At the same time, the regions left out of the technological revolution have seen their productive potential exhausted for other reasons: under pressure of exploding demand, much of sub-Saharan Africa has abandoned the practice of crop rotation that allowed soil fertility to be restored in the absence of fertilizer. Elsewhere, overgrazing is causing serious damage to the vegetal cover. Finally, demographic growth, poverty, and the absence of substitute energy policies are increasing the demand for fuel woods, leading to a sometimes irreversible degradation of the forest cover. Such practices speed up the process of aridification under way throughout the Sahel region.

Two schools of thought are at odds today in the field of agriculture. Partisans of a "green super-revolution" see the pursuit of technological progress and genetic engineering as the only possible response to the rise in demand and pay little attention to the dangers of exhausting the world's productive potential: the new genetically modified food plants represent the panacea of the twenty-first century. But before they can prove their usefulness, these plants run the risk of further degrading the biodiversity already at risk, without reducing the nutrition shortages of the farm populations of the Southern Hemisphere—for those farmers the plants will remain financially out of reach.

Other researchers urge the implementation of a "double-green revolution." This new agricultural revolution will supposedly meet the dual challenge of being more productive and still "greener" than the first one. It will indeed have to meet a considerable growth in demand, but it also faces the new task of natural resource conservation and pollution limits. In addition, contrary to the revolution of the 1960s that largely ignored needs of rural populations, this second revolution will aim to ensure food security for everyone.

Agricultural policies that deal with both the increasing immediate needs and the preservation of natural resources to meet needs in the long term are not at all utopian. But in the countries of the Northern Hemisphere as well as the Southern, these policies will require a radical change in current thinking. Thanks to the slowing of demographic growth and to reasonable expectations (although not assurances) of progress from agronomical research, the world is not in danger of starvation—on two conditions: a rapid reduction in the inequalities that are the main cause of hunger today; and a refusal to yield to the folly of short-term profitability, which could compromise the ability to feed the 8 billion to 10 billion of us who will live on the earth tomorrow.

Sophie Bessis

p. 337
SPIRE OF THE CHRYSLER BUILDING, New York, United States
In the heart of the borough of Manhattan, in New York City, rises the Chrysler Building. The spire, made up of a series of superimposed steel arches, reflects the rays of the sun by day and is illuminated at night. Architect William Van Alen designed this Art Deco building on the orders of automobile magnate Walter P. Chrysler. At 77 stories and 1,050 feet (319 m) high, it was the tallest building in New York when it opened in 1930; but it was dethroned by the Empire State Building, which rises 1,250 feet (381 m), in 1931. The Chrysler still counts among the city's forty tallest skyscrapers, all of which are above 655 feet (200 m) in height. The demographic and economic growth of the world's megalopolises inspires buildings of ever-growing height. The record in the year 2000 is held by the Nina Tower in Hong Kong, which is 1,705 feet (520 m) tall.

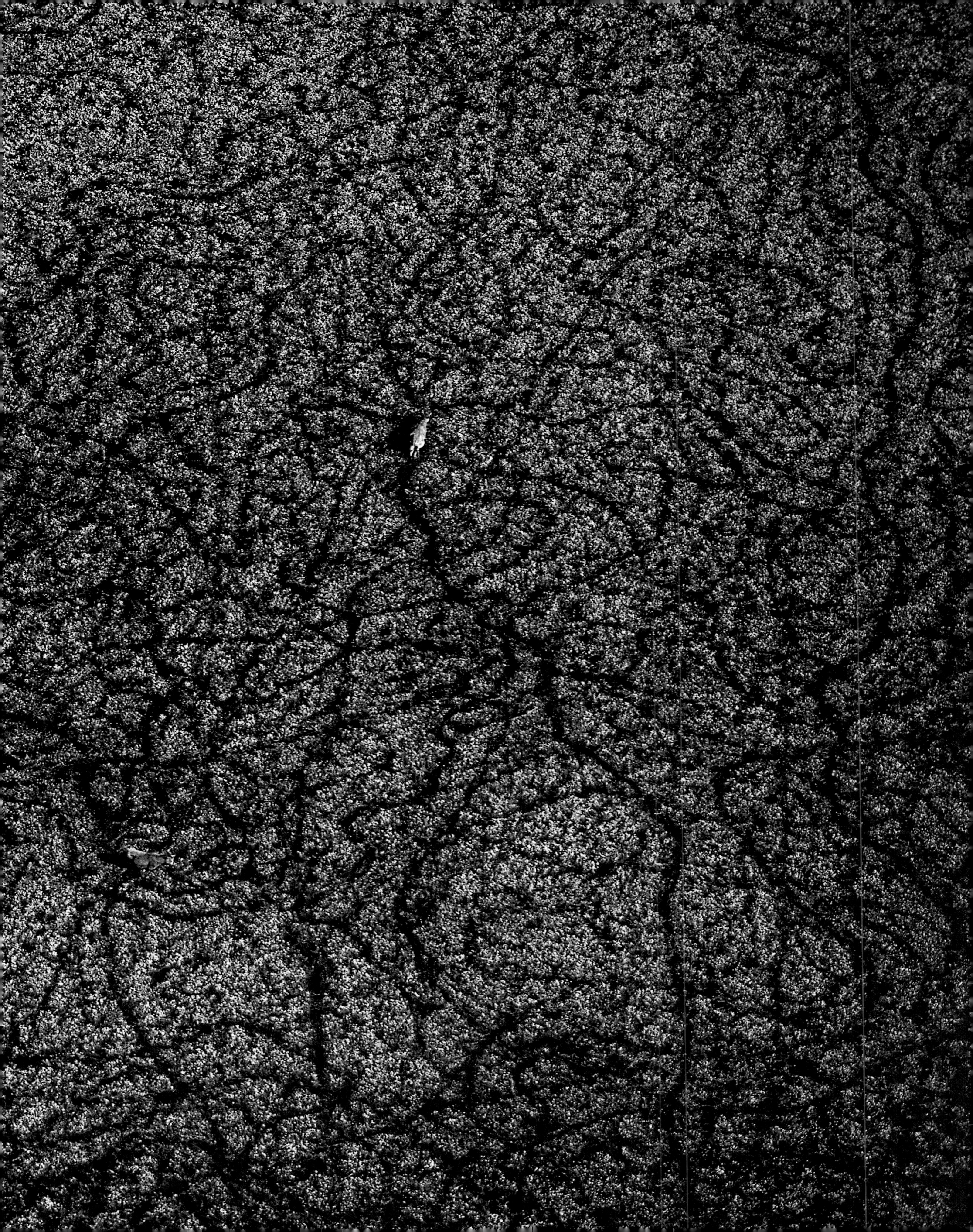

ENDANGERED CLIMATES

Little exists in our own personal experience to suggest that climate can vary significantly over the long term, even if we know that the Sahara once knew a relatively humid climate and that Scandinavia at one time lay buried under two to three kilometers of ice. The variation in past climates is explained basically by astronomical causes. But now a new actor has appeared on the scene of climatic change: humanity itself.

Our daily perception concerns temperature, rain, or wind in the course of days or seasons. These short-term fluctuations are matters of meteorology. Contrary to the variable nature of daily weather, the Sahara, Amazon, and the Siberian taiga are natural regions associated with a certain image of stability and regularity in meteorological conditions and the very notion of climate. Climatology concerns itself with evolutions in the "average" meteorological conditions over long periods (multiple decades, centuries). Thus, the word *climate* evokes a set of natural conditions over the course of centuries, leaving a sustained impression on populations in a particular region of the world.

THE ATMOSPHERE AND THE GREENHOUSE EFFECT

The sun is the source of energy for the climatic engine. Energy received by the earth is sent toward space, but only after it has undergone numerous transformations, the global balance of which is known as the toll of radiation. The atmosphere redistributes heat surpluses from the tropical regions toward the higher latitudes. The oceans, which cover 71 percent of the earth's surface, also take part in this redistribution, by means of two essential mechanisms: the marine currents (such as the Gulf Stream) and evaporation, which initiates the water cycle.

About 30 percent of solar energy reaching the borders of the atmosphere is directly reflected into space by clouds and dust. An additional 23 percent of this solar energy is absorbed by the atmosphere, and 47 percent reaches the earth's surface. The atmosphere can be permeated by radiation received from the visible light of the sun. In contrast, the radiation reemitted by the earth is conveyed essentially in infrared form. The earth's atmosphere strongly reabsorbs this radiation by way of water vapor and carbon dioxide, as well as through other gases that it contains in very small quantities. These molecules play a role comparable to that of a glass greenhouse by allowing the sunlight to pass through while retaining the reemitted infrared rays of the earth. This is the "greenhouse effect." Without this effect, the earth would probably be uninhabitable, because its average temperature would be approximately −4° F (−20° C) rather than 49° F (15° C). The increase in this greenhouse effect because of human action is at the center of current debates on future climatic changes.

p. 368
MINARET OF THE GREAT MOSQUE OF AGADEZ, Aïr Mountains, Niger
The Great Mosque of Agadez was built in the sixteenth century, at a time when the city was at the height of its power. This dried-earth building in the Sudanese style is crowned with a pyramid-shaped minaret that is 90 feet (27 m) high, bristling with thirteen rows of stakes that reinforce the fragile structure and serve as scaffolding for the periodic restoration of its surface. Agadez, known as the "gate to the desert," is the last major settlement before the Sahara and an important commercial center. It stands at the intersection of important trans-Saharan caravan routes. It is one of the holy cities of Islam, and its population is predominantly Muslim, as is 99 percent of Niger. Islam has more than 1.1 billion followers worldwide, the second-largest religion following in the world.

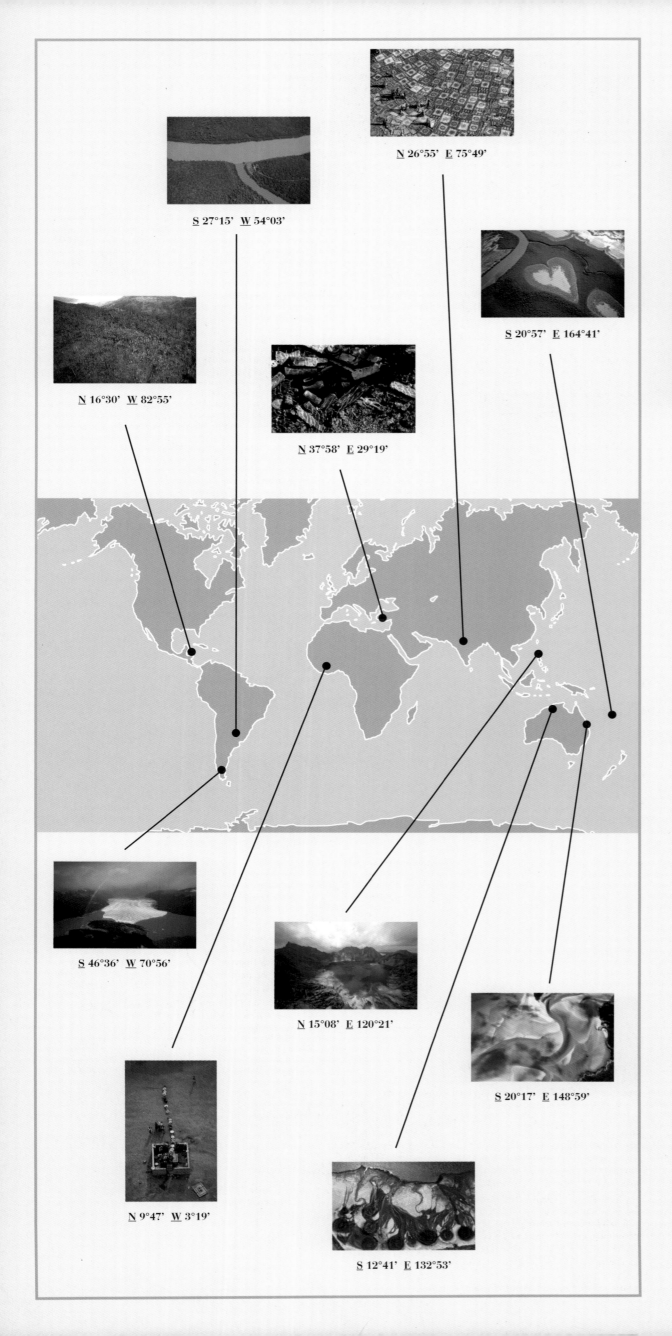

N 26°55' E 75°49'

S 27°15' W 54°03'

S 20°57' E 164°41'

N 16°30' W 82°55'

N 37°58' E 29°19'

S 46°36' W 70°56'

N 15°08' E 120°21'

S 20°17' E 148°59'

N 9°47' W 3°19'

S 12°41' E 132°53'

...mperatures and in their inertia. In addi-
...mpact of the atmosphere shows that the
...ally heated from below. In fact, it draws
...ergy from direct rays of the sun, 22 per-
...gy reemitted by the continents, and the
...nt from the energy from the oceans, pri-
...er evaporation.

...e main source of energy for the atmo-
...nd energy vector, the well for carbon diox-
...master of climatic change on every scale

...e, atmospheric and oceanic circulations
...ry different scales. They range from dis-
...d disappearing within a few days to sea-
...weather for the atmosphere, from equa-
...nts that change with the rhythm of the
...low circulation of deep waters, whose typ-
...thousand years.

...overlook the more local variations linked
...particular the consequences of changes
...in which the vapor present in the air is
...mponents of the greenhouse effect. The
...sed by human societies has tripled in the
...rimarily on account of increased irriga-
...represents 10 percent of the drainage

waters, which are almost directly evapor

gation is employed mainly in the warm re

where the air is far from the threshold

This vapor, drawn toward higher latitudes

cover. The water cycle has also been affec

tion of forests, whose role as humidity re

ing along with the process of tropical de

These issues prompt scientific ques

tions of climate in the twenty-first centu

are leading to various important climatic

lems cannot be reduced to the emission of

global warming, which are practically

raised and discussed in major internatio

CLIMATIC CHANGE AND HUMAN RESPONSIBILITY

There is no doubt that a climatic

geopolitical consequence is under way

responsibility is heavily involved, throug

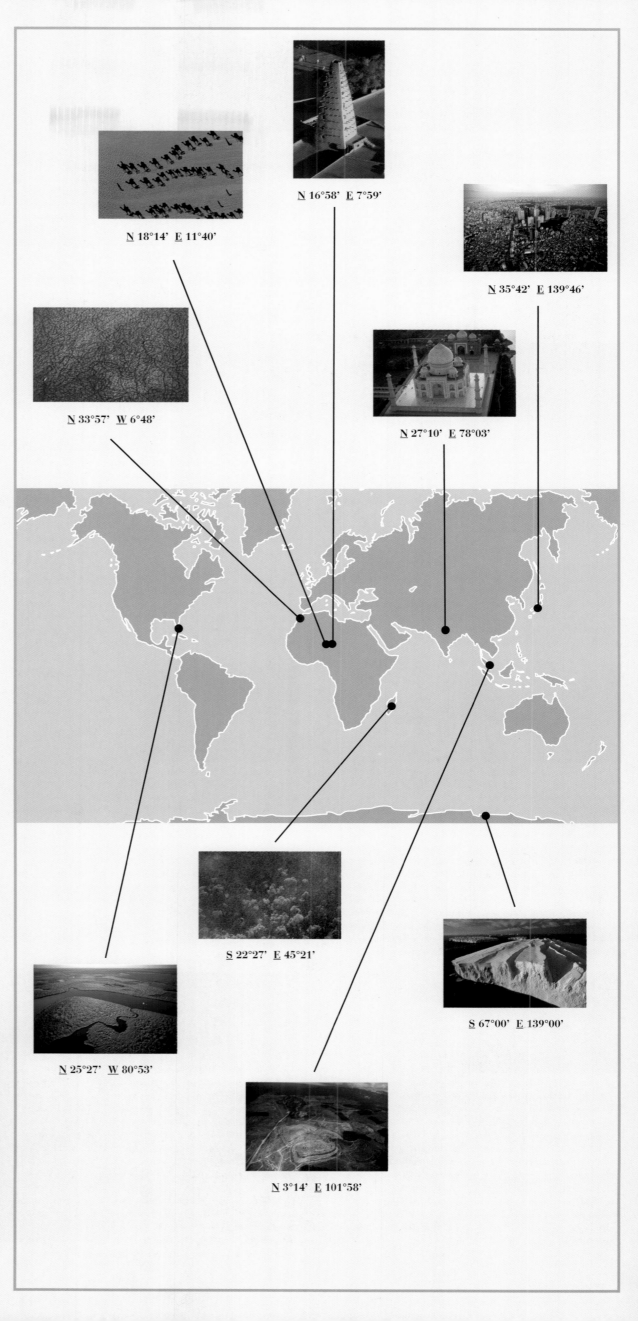

N 18°14' E 11°40'

N 16°58' E 7°59'

N 35°42' E 139°46'

N 33°57' W 6°48'

N 27°10' E 78°03'

S 22°27' E 45°21'

N 25°27' W 80°53'

S 67°00' E 139°00'

N 3°14' E 101°58'

Although many uncertainties still persist, the effects of these changes on a planet that is already badly off could clearly assume catastrophic dimensions, with a multiplication of these extreme climatic conditions. On the eve of the twenty-first century, nineteen countries—particularly in the Middle East and the Maghreb—already suffer from drought, and their number will probably double by the year 2025. In Africa aridity will especially affect the fringes of the Sahel, as well as the west and south of the continent. Southern Europe will also undergo a reduction in rain, from 20 percent (in winter) to 30 percent (in summer), while the northwest of the continent could see rains and the risk of floods increase, similar to those that ravaged the plains alongside the Oder and Neisse Rivers of Eastern Europe in July 1997. A comparable scenario could occur in Australia, where the immense central desert might become increasingly arid, while the coastal regions that today receive the most precipitation could experience diluvial rains.

Thus, the extremes of today's earth are becoming intensified: the drop in temperature of the polar night above the Arctic Ocean; the increasing violence of El Niño and La Niña above the South Pacific and of tropical hurricanes.

The Restriction and Prevention of Major Risks

The scientific debates continue as to the precise amplitude of the climatic changes, but their global impact is without doubt. On average, the climatic shifts toward the poles and mountain peaks are 95 miles (150 km) toward the north

and 500 feet (150 m) toward the summit, respectively, per degree of temperature increase. Some vegetable species cannot survive the speed of this change and will disappear.

Global warming can also directly affect human health. According to a report of the World Health Organization (WHO) published in 1996, a rise in the average earth temperature of 9° F (5° C) could allow malaria to spread an additional 7 million square miles (17 million km²)—about twice the area of Europe—endangering 60 percent of the world population, as opposed to 45 percent today. Mediterranean Europe and the southwestern states of the United States are already regions of concern. The WHO also foresees the spread of other tropical illnesses, such as yellow fever and sleeping sickness.

The importance of climatic risks justifies intensified scientific research as well as serious dissemination of information among citizens—and it also demands action.

Jean-Paul Deléage

---

p. 377
HYDRAULIC DRILLING STATION IN A VILLAGE NEAR DOROPO,
Bouna region, Côte d'Ivoire
All over Africa, the task of collecting water is assigned to women, as seen here in northern Côte d'Ivoire. Hydraulic drilling stations, equipped with pumps that are usually manual, are gradually replacing the traditional village wells, and containers of plastic, enameled metal, or aluminum are supplanting canaris (large terracotta jugs) and gourds for transporting the the precious resource. The water of these pits is more sanitary that that of traditional wells, 70 percent of which is unfit for drinking. At the dawn of the year 2000, three-quarters of the earth's inhabitants lack running water. Approximately 1.6 billion people have no drinkable water, and illnesses from unhealthy water are the major cause of infant mortality in developing nations.

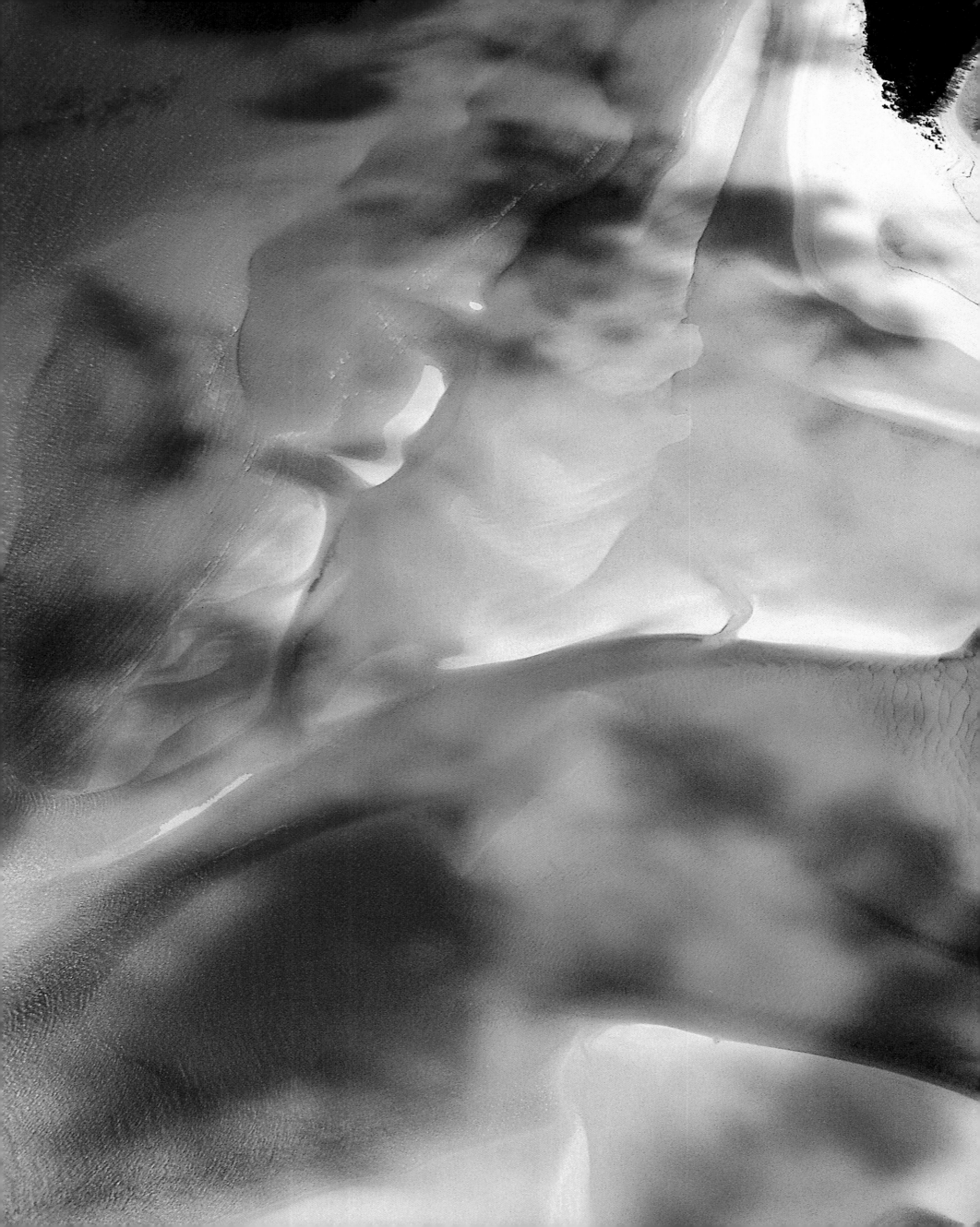

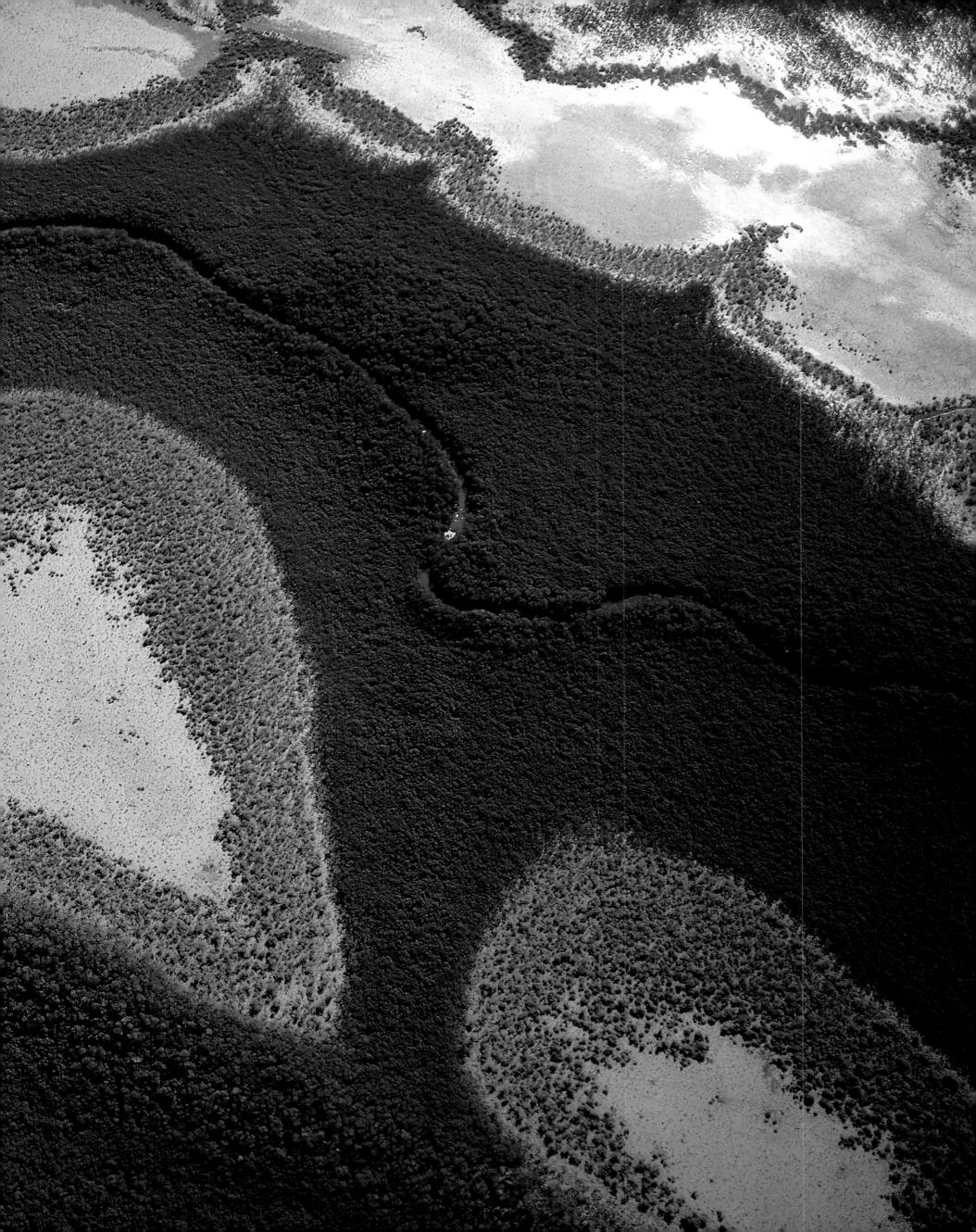

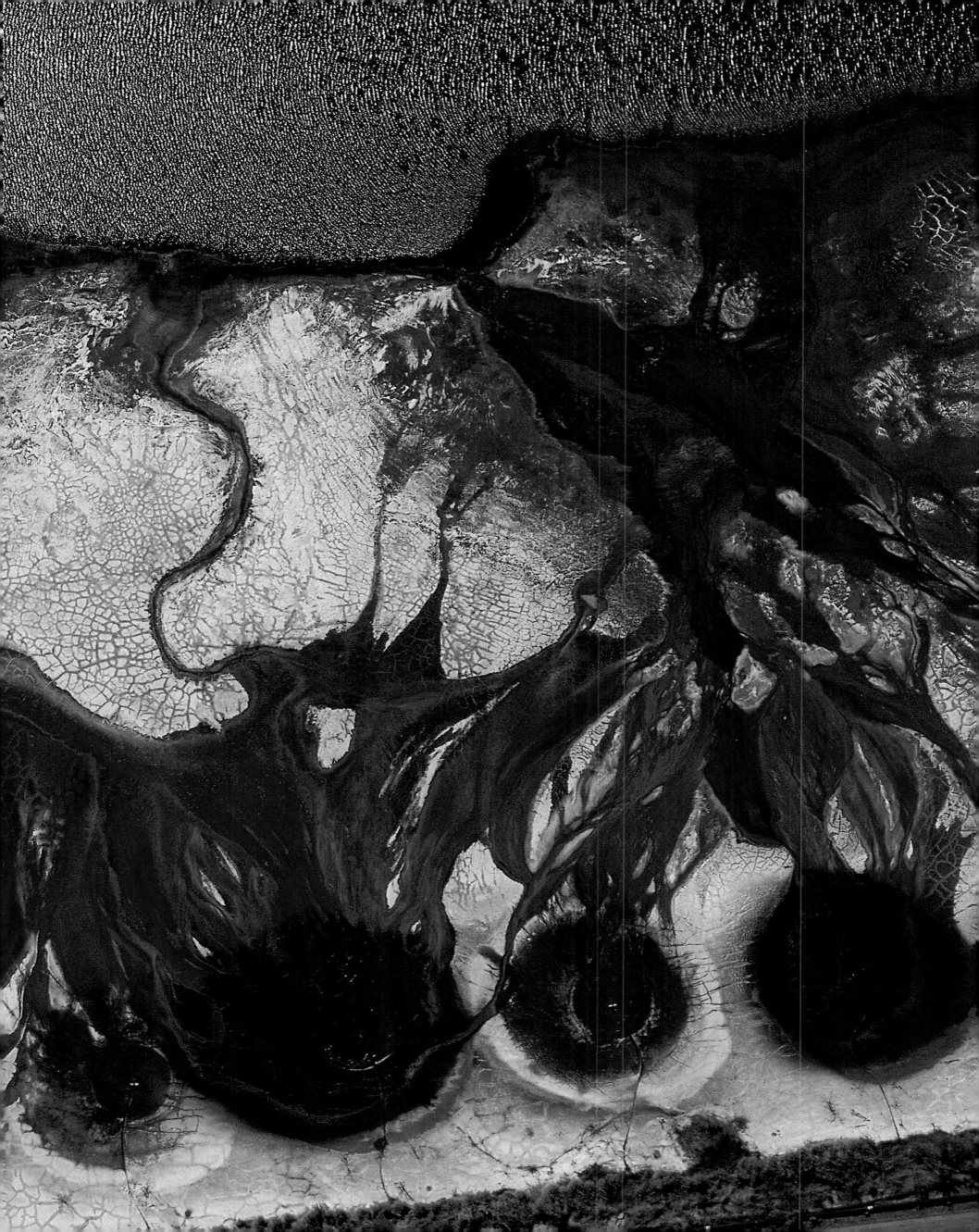

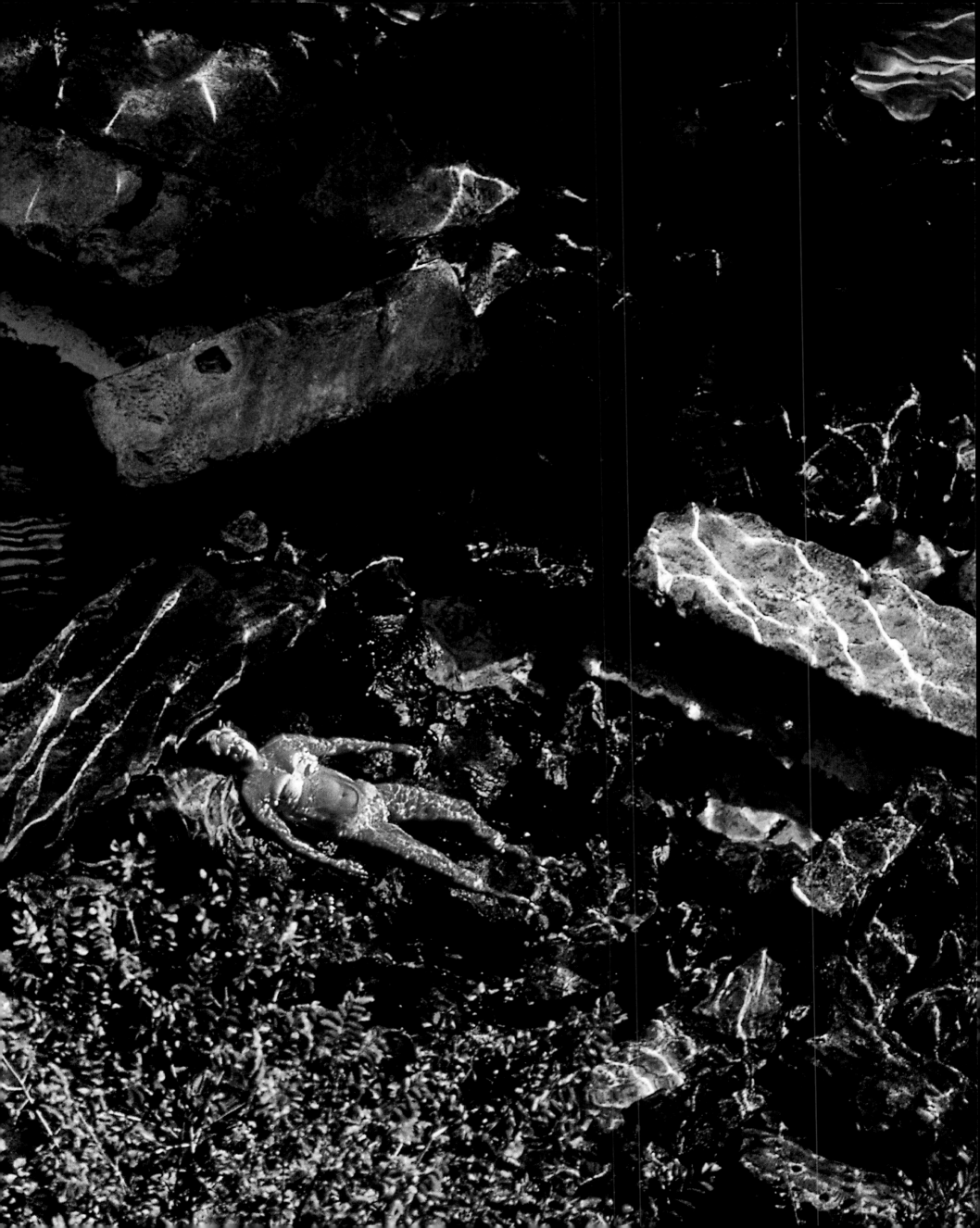

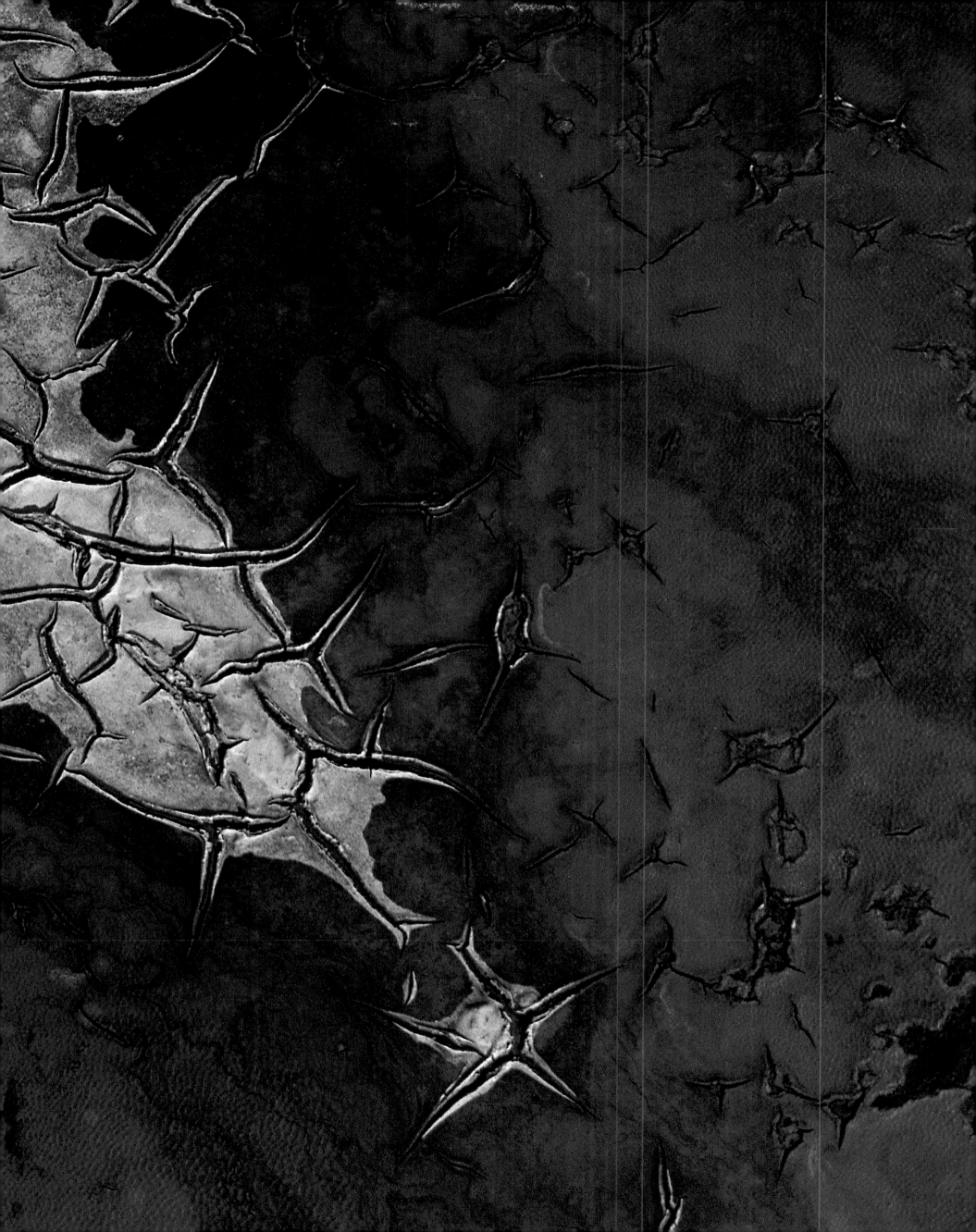

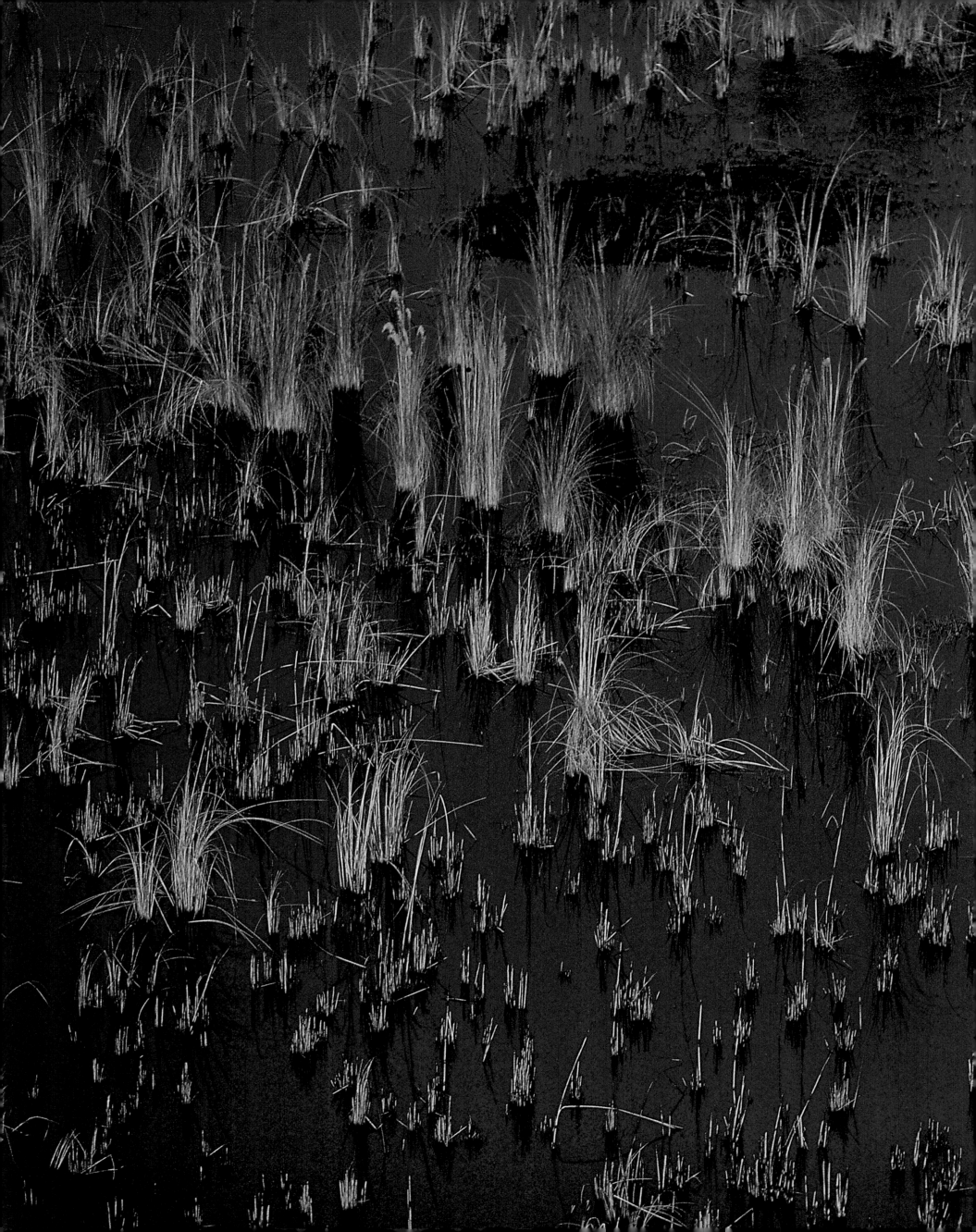

TOWARD A SUSTAINABLE DEVELOPMENT

The "Earth Summit" at Rio in 1992 focused its concerns on the conditions required for a "sustainable development" by making a close association between the environment and development. According to the report *Our Common Future*, published in 1987 in preparation for the Rio meeting, the aim was "to make development sustainable—to ensure that it meets the needs of the present without compromising the ability of future generations to meet their own needs."

These conditions presuppose several actions. The first is to prioritize the urgency of environmental risks; the second is to define concrete commitments needed in order to avoid the worst disasters; the third is to identify the resources that wealthy nations in particular ought to devote to the realization of these commitments; the fourth and final initiative is to evaluate the changes called for in this new form of development.

These proposals are based on one implicit assumption: the *un*sustainability of the present type and speed of growth. The earth's resources are not inexhaustible; the biosphere constitutes a finite world, and the human species has already dealt it irreparable blows. Can economic development occur without endangering our natural heritage? How can this need be met while still providing for the vital needs of all people?

THE MIRAGE OF CATCH-UP THEORY

We must first understand the dynamics of demographic growth in order to master its consequences better. The world population is growing by approximately 80 million people each year, and 80 percent of that growth occurs in developing nations. Data from the United Nations Food and Agricultural Organization (FAO) indicate that 800 million people around the world suffer from malnutrition, and 13 million children under five years of age die each year from the direct results of malnutrition or from illnesses linked to it; the World Health Organization (WHO) reports that 1.8 billion people lack healthy drinking water.

It is also crucial to modify the current trends of economic development and the distribution of wealth between the Northern and Southern Hemispheres, as well as within each hemisphere. This will oblige us to give up a popular tenet that

continues to inspire many visions of the future: the catch-up theory, which states that the benefits of uninterrupted economic growth cannot fail to reach all of humanity by trickling down from the top of societies. If we wanted to guarantee the 6 billion inhabitants of the earth in the year 2000 the income of the American middle class, the flow of resources consumed by the world economic engine would have to be multiplied by a factor of about five. It would have to be still higher if we wanted to ensure this catch-up effect for the 9 billion to 11 billion who will occupy the planet by the mid-twenty-first century.

The catch-up theory is even more untenable if we consider the new ecological constraints. If countries can only catch up with the wealthiest by imitating their development model, this attempt will run into insurmountable difficulties long before attaining success. This applies above all to the degradation of natural resources.

Extraordinary economic growth is enjoyed today by just over one-third of humanity, and it remains a hope for the other two-thirds. Near the end of the eighteenth century, the gap in the standard of living between Europeans and the rest of the world did not exceed the level of 2 to 1; by the beginning of the twentieth century, this ratio was nearly 10 to 1. According to a computation by the United Nations Development Program (UNDP), the richest 20 percent of the world population in 1960 had an income 30 times higher than that of the poorest 20 percent. By the mid-1980s, the same source placed this ratio at 60 to 1.

THE NORTH-SOUTH GAP

We cannot plan a sustainable growth that would not be equitable. The call for a sustainable development thus means not only the preservation of resources and a livable environment for our children and grandchildren; it also signifies the correction of this historic tendency to widen inequalities. We must work for a development that is humane and equal.

Attempts have been made to estimate, in concrete financial terms, the implementation of such a form of development. At the Copenhagen Summit of 1995 devoted to social development, the UNDP estimated this cost at an annual total of at least $40 billion, covering four priorities: education, population, health, and access to drinking water. According to the recommendations of Agenda 21 (thus named because of the twenty-one main recommendations made by the Rio

Conference in 1992), a total of $120 bill
be devoted each year to a humane developr
environmental demands. But these figure
unless they are seen in the wider context o
the Northern and Southern Hemispheres.

In the Northern Hemisphere the envire
massive pollution effects are directly trace
sive gains in the production of consume
since the end of World War II. In contras
Hemisphere the destruction of the enviror
price exacted by misery and poverty. These
tries, following the lead of the industrializ
utilize their labor force while overexploi
resources: mines, forests, soils, coastlines. T
enormous national debts, and an essen
exports must go to paying off these debts

The environmental crisis presents it
cal terms. Undoubtedly, the ailments unle
by an economic system that seeks produc
any price are universal in nature. But in th
sphere the dominant problem is a crisis of
the Southern Hemisphere, as well as increa
hundreds of millions of people are unable

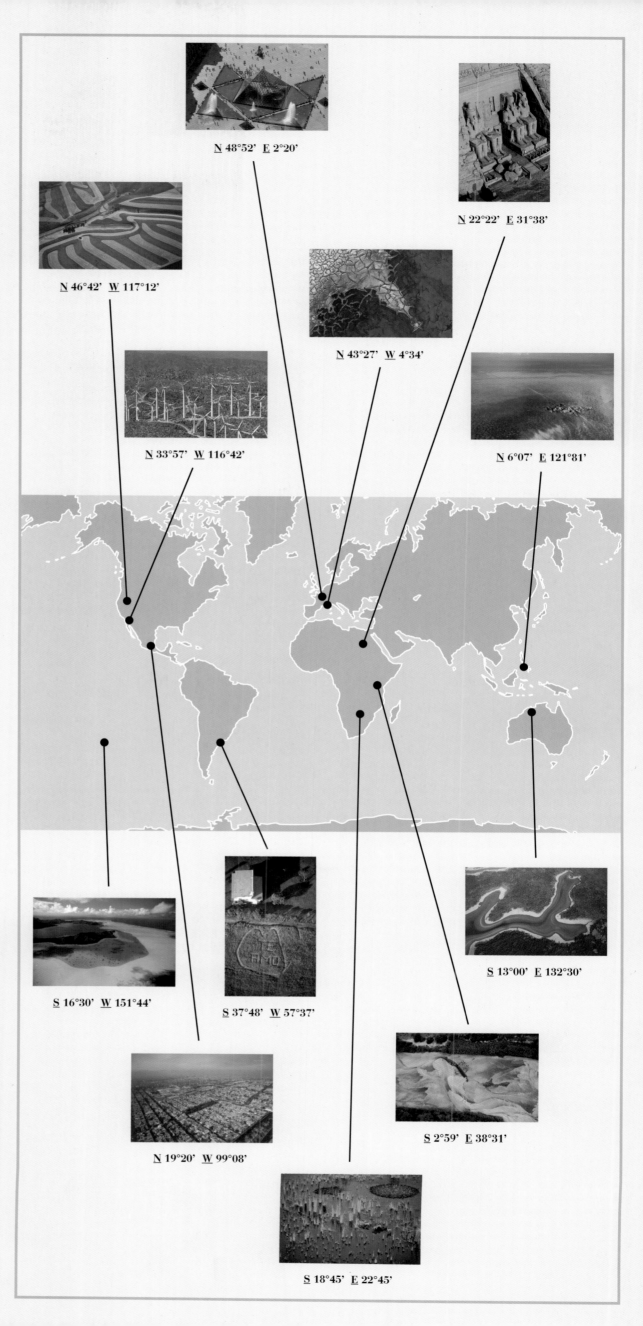

N 48°52' E 2°20'

N 22°22' E 31°38'

N 46°42' W 117°12'

N 43°27' W 4°34'

N 33°57' W 116°42'

N 6°07' E 121°81'

S 16°30' W 151°44'

S 37°48' W 57°37'

S 13°00' E 132°30'

N 19°20' W 99°08'

S 2°59' E 38°31'

S 18°45' E 22°45'

exerted on the biosphere. Numerous courses of action have been proposed with a view to making a simultaneous attack on the problems of poverty and the environment: increased efforts in the recycling of materials and reduced energy consumption; support for small-scale peasant farming; development of social services and education; and public works to improve national infrastructures.

We already know the potential sources of financing for these projects. An eco-tax of one dollar per barrel of petroleum would correspond to $60 billion per year. The proposal by Nobel Prize laureate James Tobin to levy a 0.05 percent tax on speculative profits on currency transactions in cash could bring in $150 billion per year. And setting aside 0.7 percent of the gross national product of industrialized nations to aid the development of southern countries would amount to approximately $140 billion per year.

The question, then, is whether the industrial world has the political will for this implementation. The wealthiest societies are reticent when faced with the financial contributions demanded of them, whereas the poorest nations have difficulty accepting restrictions imposed on them when they remain excluded from the amenities of mass consumption.

The objective of a sustainable development will have to be pursued on the transnational level. The Gordian knot of the environmental question can be solved only by a true reversal of our historical relationship to the environment. A new system of governability for our planet must emerge from a new ethic of planetary solidarity and responsibility toward future generations. Today the crisis of the environment and development puts the future of humanity at risk. At this time, we must renew the inspirational hope of the UN Charter, which opens with this great formulation: "We the peoples of the United Nations."

Jean-Paul Deléage

HELICOPTER NEAR KORHOGO,
Côte d'Ivoire

INDEX

AFTERWORD: THE STORY OF A BOOK

Children in the Philippines pose with the helicopter that has landed in their school courtyard, waiting for favorable weather conditions.

A huge map of the world covers an entire office wall. It is dotted with cardboard arrows—red for places that have been photographed, blue for those still to be shot. Black dots set off the countries that are still resisting Yann Arthus-Bertrand, although they haven't convinced him to give up the pursuit. "With him," one of his assistants will tell you, "I learned that nothing is impossible. People tell him 'No,' and he hears 'Maybe.' In the end he always gets what he wants."

In this manner, often at a forced march, the photographer has pushed ahead a colossal project that unites his love of nature, his ecological consciousness, and his fascination with photography.

His first love, for animals, drew him to Kenya after working as director of a game preserve in central France. With his wife, Anne, he spent two years photographing a family of lions. To

Logistical problems are solved with a satellite telephone.

finance the study, Yann led tourist excursions above the brush in a hot-air balloon. This experience led to his passion for aerial photography. The idea for the current project took shape gradually in the course of his travels, as this bird-man sharpened his vision and clarified his demands. "I've always wanted to give some meaning to my work," he explains. "When I started taking pictures, I set out right away to build my own subjects in a conscious effort to

get beyond the anecdotal. I have the good fortune to have a wonderful job, and I'm happy if I can share what I see from up high. For me, a photographer is not an artist. Artists transform reality. I'm the exact opposite: I try not to transform it."

Aerial photography requires a great deal of organization. The way Yann Arthus-Bertrand goes about it, it demands dynamism and persistence. In the case of *Earth from Above*, the job took a tremendous amount of energy. Once the master plan was established, the task was to translate it into reality—which meant acquiring the means to realize it. UNESCO was very prompt to offer its sponsorship, a valuable source of support that opened quite a few doors. Then along came Fuji in Japan, Corbis in the United States and, lastly, Air France, who provided the airline tickets. This assistance meant the beginning of an adventure that had no room for amateurism and improvisation.

A whole team took shape around Yann Arthus-Bertrand to ensure the preparation and management of his missions. This was a long-term undertaking. The final tally would be five years of work, 2,000 flight hours, several trips around the world, 15,000 rolls of film, and some 100,000 photographs that were winnowed down to the number in this book: 195 shots taken from the sky over 75 countries.

In the "Earth from Above" headquarters in Paris, a vast ground-floor studio in the 15th Arrondissement, the world map studded with arrows rises above a desk with an open atlas. Everywhere are light tables for viewing slides, filing cases, shelves loaded with geography and economics texts, travel volumes, guides, maps and plans, encyclopedias, magazines. A collection of miniature biplanes and helicopters made of wire and spools, collected from all over the globe, stands on top of the cabinets. Half-hidden in a dark corner is a large naive painting of Yann in his helicopter, above a peaceful beach—a work blissfully ignorant of all the complex, precise operations organized by this agency.

In Namibia, a Himba woman asks Yann to fly over her village.

Accompanying the quest for financing is the grueling job of setting up an assignment. This labyrinth of petitions and approvals can get bogged down for months at a time, especially when trying to photograph a "sensitive" country, which considers any flight over its territory a possible spy mission. Once this obstacle is overcome, the production crew swings into action. They don't follow, they lead the way. Every problem must have a solution. It might be a matter of scouring the backest of backwaters for a helicopter that is dexterous, light, and preferably lent by the government of the region to save on rental fees (between $1,000 and $4,000 an hour). Or else the crew must bring a helicopter into the selected site if none is locally available. At all times everyone is in unbearable suspense about the weather. Staying in close touch with the French weather service Météo France Internationale, the team keeps fine-tuning the forecasts. A mission can be canceled at the very last minute after months of preparation, because aerial photographs demand a very clear sky. In addition,

Above Mount Everest, at 16,500 feet, oxygen is necessary.

Yann prefers warm lighting. At daybreak he starts a two-hour shooting session, then comes back for more pictures two or three hours before sunset. He is also fond of streaked skies or the clearing after a storm. He avoids working in broad daylight in the glaring sun, except for shots of ocean floors, which need the fullest lighting.

The insecurity of the Borneo region in the Philippines makes it necessary for the team to carry arms.

When everything works to perfection, and Yann comes home with just what he wanted, the job is still not yet finished. The publication rights remain to be negotiated. Just before this book went to press, the photograph of a slaughterhouse was censored, on the ground that it presented a poor image of the country in question.

For five years, Yann crisscrossed our planet for half of every month, trailing its miraculous diversity, which he is summing up now for the generations of the third millennium. "I never could have done it without the support of my family, who put up with seeing me less often, especially my wife, who took care of the things that needed to be done while I was away. And the final product reflects the efforts of the people who work with me." A twinkle in his eye, and with a sly grin, he concedes that he can be

In Bangladesh, a Swiss hydroplane is used during the floods.

difficult for his team to put up with: "I'm a bit of a loudmouth." He has special praise for his assistants: "They play a special role. They prepare everything. They carry the equipment. They take the notes. They do the captions. And since I take so many photos from the helicopter, they have to keep track of the hardware." That means six 24 x 36 cameras with ten lenses and three medium-size cameras, which have to be kept fully loaded at all times. Plus the polarizing filters, a spot meter, a small video camera, the map for staying on course, and the GPS (Global Positioning System) that pinpoints the helicopter's location within 20 meters.

Two assistants work in tandem. While one of them goes with Yann, the other looks after the shots from the previous flight and sets up the next trip. The film development phase,

which includes selecting the photos, writing the captions, and entering them in the database, can take three weeks for a fourteen-day shoot. The assistants have a homemade flight log, updated during the mission, which includes a detailed checklist with one puzzling entry: "Keep on hand: red clothing for photos." To catch the full sense of an aerial shot the viewer must grasp the dimensions of what is shown and the distances involved. When no reference point exists, the assistant, dropped on the ground and nicely visible in red, provides a sense of scale.

"The assistant has to be crazy about photography," Yann observes. "And someone I like." His co-workers feel the same way about him, stern taskmaster that he is. "He demands so much that, sometimes—especially in the begin-

The most uncomfortable part of aerial photography is the cold—the helicopter door is never closed during the flight.

ning—you can run yourself ragged. But you learn fast." They make up a close-knit group, loyal, with a sense of family, inspired by the scope of their project, especially high-spirited when it comes to poring over contact proofs after each new mission to find the best shots. The real plums, known as "calendar shots," make up the raw material for the calendar that the agency has created every year since 1994. Down at the corner bistro, Chez Gérard, the team has a regular table. With the daily special

in front of them, they keep up a familiar refrain: "Yann shows us things we couldn't have seen on our own. He has a graphic eye." Yann always denies it: "If there's art in my pictures, that's only because it exists in nature, because the world is art."

"From up above," he adds, "there's no difference between the city and nature. The city is a composite made up of different pieces of nature." No complete divorce exists between the human animal and its territory.

Traveling around the world and witnessing its splendors, Yann says that has come to feel the world's fragility. This book, he hopes, will help in some small way to raise awareness of the dangers caused by population growth and by the powers of destruction the human species has

Yann explains his flight over Madagascar to village children on the island.

now attained. These photographs are just the first phase of a project, and perhaps they will inspire more companies and more people to join in.

A minute later the photographer shows how, in the helicopter, he uses gestures to guide the pilot toward the angle he wants. His hands fly about like those of an orchestra conductor. In images, he is composing his own "Song of the Earth."

Joëlle Ody

The *Earth from Above* team (left to right): Franck Charel, photo assistant; Isabelle Lechenet, illustration documentation; Catherine Arthus-Bertrand, exhibition coordination; Françoise Le Roch'Briquet, editorial coordination; Hélène de Bonis, production coordination; Françoise Jacquot and Christophe Daguet, photo assistants. (Missing from the photo: Florence Frutoso)

ACKNOWLEDGMENTS

UNESCO: Federico Mayor, Director General; Pierre Lasserre, Director of the Divison of Ecological Sciences; Mireille Jardin, Jane Robertson, Josette Gainche and Malcolm Hadley, Hélène Gosselin, Carlos Marquès, Mr. Oudatchine of the Office of Public Information; Francesco di Castri and Jeanne Barbière, of the Environmental Coordination division

FUJIFILM: Masayuki Muneyuki, President, Toshiyuki "Todd" Hirai, and Minoru "Mick" Uranaka of Fujifilm in Tokyo; Peter Samwell of Fujifilm Europe; Doris Goertz, Ms. Develey, Marc Héraud, Jean-Pierre Colly, François Rychelewski, Bruno Baudry, Hervé Chanaud, Franck Portelance, Piotr Fedorowicz, Françoise Moumaneix, and Anissa Auger of Fujifilm France

CORBIS: Stephen B. Davis, Peter Howe, Graham Cross, Charles Mauzy, Vanessa Kramer, Tana Wollen, and Vicky Whiley

AIR FRANCE: François Brousse and Christine Micouleau, Mireille Queillé and Bodo Ravoninjatovo

As we complete this final page, mindful of so many good memories from evey corner of the planet, our only fear is that we may have forgotten one of the many people who have helped us to realize this project. We sincerely apologize for any such oversight, and we assure you of our heartfelt gratitude.

ALBANIA
ECPA, Lieutenant Colonel Aussavy
DICOD, Colonel Baptiste, Captain Maranzana, and Captain Saint-Léger
SIRPA, Charles-Philippe d'Orléans
DETALAT, Captain Ludovic Janot
Staffs of the French air force, Etienne Hoff, Cyril Vasquèz, Olivier Ouakel, José Trouille, Frédéric Le Mouillour, François Dughin, Christian Abgral, Patric Comerier, Guillaume Maury, Franck Novak, pilots

ANTARCTICA
Institut Français pour la Recherche et la Technologie Polaires, Gérard Jugie
L'Astrolabe, Captain Gérard R. Daudon, Sd Capitaine Alain Gaston
Heli Union France, Bruno Fiorese, pilot
Augusto Leri and Mario Zucchelli, Projetto Antartida, Italy
Terra Nova

ARGENTINA
Jean-Louis Larivière, Ediciones Larivière
Mémé and Marina Larivière, Felipe C. Larivière
Dudú von Thielman
Virginia Taylor of Fernández Beschtedt
Commander Sergio Copertari, pilot; Emilio Yañez and Pedro Diamante, co-pilots; Eduardo Benítez, mechanic
Squadron of Federal Air Police, Commissioner Norberto Edgardo Gaudiero
Captain Roberto A. Ulloa, former governor of the province of Salta
Orán precinct house, Salta province, Commander Daniel D. Pérez
Military Geograpical Institute
Commissioner Rodolfo E. Pantanali
Aerolineas Argentinas

AUSTRALIA
Helen Hiscocks
Australian Tourism Commission, Kate Kenward, Paul Gauger, and Gemma Tisdell
Jairow Helicopters
Heliwork, Simon Eders
Thai Airways, Pascale Baret
Club Meds of Lindeman Island and Byron Bay Beach

BAHAMAS
Club Meds of Eleuthera, Paradise

BANGLADESH
Hossain Kommol and Salahuddin Akbar, External Publicity Wing of the Ministry of Foreign Affairs, Dacca
His Excellency Tufail K. Haider, ambassador of Bangladesh in Paris, and Chowdhury Ikthiar, first secretary
Her Excellency Renée Veyret, ambassador of France in Dacca
Mohamed Ali and Amjad Hussain of Biman Bangladesh Airlines, Vishawjeet
Mr. Nakada, Fujifilm in Singapore
Mr. Ezaher of the Fujifilm laboratory, Dacca
Mizanur Rahman, director, Rune Karlsson, pilot, and Eldon, mechanic, MAF Air Support
Muhiuddin Rashida, Sheraton Hotel, Dacca
Mr. Minto

BOTSWANA
Maas Müller, Chobe Helicopter

BRAZIL
Governor of Mato Grosso do Norte e do Sul
Fundação Pantanal, Erasmo Machado Filho, and the Regional Natural Parks of France, Emmanuel Thévenin and Jean-Luc Sadorge
Fernando Lemos
His Excellency Mr. Pedreira, Brazilian ambassador to UNESCO
Dr. Iracema Alencar de Queiros, Instituto de Proteção Ambiental do Amazonas, and his son Alexandro
Brasília Tourism Office
Luis Carlos Burti, Editions Burti
Carlos Marquès, OPI Division, UNESCO
Ethel Leon, Anthea Communication
TV Globo
José Augusto Wanderley and Juliana Marquès of Golden Cross
Hotel Tropical, Manaus
VARIG

CANADA
Anne Zobenbuhler, Canadian Embassy in Paris and Tourism Office
Barbara di Stefano and Laurent Beunier, Destination Québec
Cherry Kemp Kinnear, Nunavut Tourism Office
Huguette Parent and Chrystiane Galland, Air Canada
First Air
Vacances Air Transat
André Buteau, pilot, Essor Helicopters
Louis Drapeau, Canadian Helicopters
Canadian Airlines

CHINA
Tourism Office, Hong Kong, Mr. Iskaros
Chinese Embassy in Paris, His Excellency Mr. Caifangbo, Li Beifen
French Embassy in Beijing, His Excellency Pierre Morel
Shi Guangeng
Serge Nègre
Yan Layma

COTE D'IVOIRE
Vitrail & Architecture, Pierre Fakhoury
Hugues Moreau and pilots Jean-Pierre Artifoni and Philippe Nallet, Ivoire Hélicoptères
Patricia Kriton and Mr. Kesada, Air Afrique

DENMARK
Weldon Owen Publishing, the entire production team of "Over Europe"

ECUADOR
Loup Langton and Pablo Corral Vega, Descubriendo Ecuador
Claude Lara, minister of foreign affairs in Ecuador
Mr. Galarza, Ecuadorian consulate, France
Eliecer Cruz, Diego Bouilla, Robert Bensted-Smith, Galapagos National Park
Patrizia Schrank, Jennifer Stone, "European Friends of Galapagos"
Danilo Matamoros, Jaime and Cesar, Taxi Aero Inter Islas M.T.B.
Etienne Moine, Latitude 0°
Abdon Guerrero, San Cristobal airport

EGYPT
Rallye des Pharaons, "Fenouil," organizer, Bernard Seguy, Michel Beaujard, and Christian Thévenet, pilots

FRANCE
Dominique Voynet, minister of land use and the environment
Defense Ministry/SIRPA
Préfecture de Police, Paris
Montblanc Hélicoptères, Franck Arrestier and Alexandre Antunes, pilots
Corsica Tourism Office, Xavier Olivieri
Departmental Tourism Committee of Auvergne, Cécile da Costa
Conseil Général of the Côtes d'Armor, Charles Josselin and Gilles Pellan
Conseil Général of Savoie, Jean-Marc Eysserick
Conseil Général of Haute-Savoie, Georges Pacquetet and Laurent Guette
Conseil Général of the Alpes-Maritimes, Sylvie Grosgojeat and Cécile Alziary
Conseil Général of Yvelines, Franck Borotra, president, Christine Boutin, Pascal Angenault, and Odile Roussillon
CDT of the Départements de la Loire
Rémy Martin, Dominique Hériard-Dubreuil
Nicole Bru
Editions du Chêne, Philippe Pierrelee, artistic director
Hachette, Jean Arcache
Moët et Chandon/Rallye GTO, Jean Berchon and Philippe des Roys du Roure
Printemps de Cahors, Marie-Thérèse Perrin
Philippe Van Montagu and Willy Gouere, pilot
SAF hélicoptères, Christophe Rosset, Hélifrance, Héli-Union, Europe
Hélicoptère Bretagne, Héli Bretagne, Héli-Océan, Héli Rhône-Alpes, Hélicos Légers

Réunion: Tourism Office of Réunion
Jean-Marie Lavèvre, pilot, Hélicoptères Helilagon
René Barrieu and Michèle Bernard
French West Indies: Club Med des Boucaniers and Club Med de la Caravelle

GREECE
Culture Ministry, Athens
Eleni Methodiou, Greek delegation to UNESCO
Hellenic Tourism Office
Club Meds of Corfu Ipsos, Gregolimano, Helios Corfu, Kos, and Olympia
Olympic Airways
INTERJET, Dimitrios Prokopis and Konstantinos Tsigkas, pilots, and Kimon Daniilidis
Meteo Center, Athens

GUATEMALA AND HONDURAS
Giovanni Herrera, director, and Carlos Llarena, pilot, Aerofoto, Guatemala City
Rafael Sagastume, STP villas, Guatemala City

ICELAND
Bergur Gislasson and Gisli Guestsson, Icephoto
Thyrluthjonustan Helicopters
Peter Samwell
National Tourism Office, Paris

INDIA
Indian embassy in Paris, His Excellency Kanwal Sibal, ambassador, Rahul Chhabra, first secretary, S. K. Sofat, general of aerial brigade, Mr. Lala, Mr. Kadyan, and Vivianne Tourtet
Ministry of foreign affairs, Teki E. Prasad and Manjish Gover
N. K. Singh, office of the Prime Minister
Mr. Chidambaram, member of parliament
Air Headquarters, S. I. Kumaran, Pande
Mandoza Air Charters, Atul Jaidka
Indian International Airways, Captain Sangha Pritvipalh
French embassy in New Delhi, His Excellency Claude Blanchemaison, ambassador, François Xavier Reymond, first secretary

INDONESIA
TOTAL Balikpapan, Ananda Idris and Ilha Sutrisno
Mr. and Mrs. Didier Millet

IRELAND
Aer Lingus
Irish National Tourism Office
Captain David Courtney, Irish Rescue Helicopters
David Hayes, Westair Aviation Ltd.

ITALY
French embassy in Rome, Michel Benard, press service
Heli Frioula, Gianfranco Greco, Stefano Fanzin, and Pierino Godicio

JAPAN
Eu Japan Festival, Shuji Kogi and Robert Delpire
Masako Sakata, IPJ
NHK TV
Japan Broadcasting Corporation

JORDAN
Ms. Sharaf, Anis Mouasher, Khaled Irani, and Khaldoun Kiwan, Royal Society for Conservation of Nature
Royal Airforces
Riad Sawalha, Royal Jordanian
Regency Palace Hotel

KAZAKHSTAN
His Excellency Nourlan Danenov, ambassador of Kazakhstan in Paris
His Excellency Alain Richard, French ambassador in Alma-Ata, and Josette Floch
Professor René Letolle
Heli Asia Air and its pilot, Mr. Anouar

KENYA
Universal Safari Tours, Nairobi, Patrix Duffar
Transsafari, Irvin Rozental

KUWAIT
Kuwait Center for Research and Studies, Prince Abdullah Al Ghunaim, Dr. Youssef
Kuwait National Commission for UNESCO, Sulaiman Al Onaizi
Kuwaiti delegation to UNESCO, His Excellency Dr. Al Salem, and Mr. Al Baghly
Kuwait Airforces, Squadron 32, Major Hussein Al-Mane, Captain Emad Al-Momen
Kuwait Airways, Mr. Al Nafisy

MADAGASCAR
Riaz Barday and Mr. Norman, pilot, Aéromarine
Sonja and Thierry Ranarivelo, Yersin Raccarlyn, pilot, Madagascar Hélicoptère
Jeff Guidez and Lisbeth

MALAYSIA
Club Med of Cherating

MALDIVES
Club Med of Faru

MALI
TSO, Rallye Dakar, Hubert Auriol
Daniel Legrand, Arpèges Conseil
Daniel Bouet, pilot of Cessna

MAURITANIA
TSO, Rallye Paris-Dakar, Hubert Auriol
Daniel Legrand, Arpèges Conseil
Daniel Bouet, pilot
Sidi Ould Kleib

MEXICO
Club Meds of Cancun, Sonora Bay, Huatulco, and Ixtapa

MOROCCO
Royal Moroccan Gendarmerie
General El Kadiri and Colonel Hamid Laanigri
François de Grossouvre

NAMIBIA
Ministry of Fisheries
French Cooperation Mission, Jean-Pierre Lahaye, Nicole Weill, Laurent Billet, and Jean Paul
Namibian Tourist Friend, Almut Steinmester

NEPAL
Nepalese embassy in Paris
Terres d'Aventure, Patrick Oudin
Great Himalayan Adventures, Ashok Basnyet
Royal Nepal Airways, J. B. Rana
Mandala Trekking, Jérôme Edou
Bhuda Air
Maison de la Chine, Patricia Tartour-Jonathan, director, Colette Vaquier and Fabienne Leriche
Marina Tymen and Miranda Ford, Cathay Pacific

NETHERLANDS
Paris Match
Franck Arrestier, pilot

NEW CALEDONIA
Charles de Montesquieu

NIGER
TSO, Rallye Paris-Dakar, Hubert Auriol
Daniel Legrand, Arpèges Conseil
Daniel Bouet, pilot of Cessna

NORWAY
Airlift A.S., Ted Juliussen, pilot, Henry Hogi, Arvid Auganaes, and Nils Myklebust

OMAN
His Majesty the Sultan Quabous ben Saïd al-Saïd
Defense Ministry, John Miller
Villa d'Alésia, William Perkins and Isabelle de Larrocha

PERU
Dr. Maria Reiche and Ana Maria Cogorno-Reiche
Ministry of foreign relations, Juan Manuel Tirado
National Police of Peru
Faucett Airline, Cecilia Raffo and Alfredo Barnechea
Eduardo Corrales, Aero Condor

PHILIPPINES
Filipino Airforces
Seven Days in the Philippines, by Editions Millet, Jill Laidlaw

PORTUGAL
Club Med of Da Balaia

POLYNESIA
Club Med of Moorea

RUSSIA
Yuri Vorobiov, vice-minister, and Mr. Brachnikov, Emerkom
Nidolai Alexiy Timochenko, Emerkom in Kamchatka
Valery Blatov, Russian delegation to UNESCO

ST. VINCENT AND THE GRENADINES
Paul Gravel, SVG Air
Jeanette Cadet, The Mustique Company
David Linley
Ali Medjahed, baker
Alain Fanchette

SENEGAL
TSO, Rallye Paris-Dakar, Hubert Auriol
Daniel Legrand, Arpèges Conseil
Daniel Bouet, pilot
Club Meds of Almadies and Cap Skirring

SOMALIA
His Royal Highness Sheikh Saud Al-Thani of Qatar
Majdi Bustami, E. A. Paulson and Osama, bureau of His Royal Highness Sheikh Saud Al-Thani
Fred Viljoen, pilot
Rachid J. Hussein, UNESCO-Peer, Hargeysa, Somalia
Nureldin Satti, UNESCO-Peer, Nairobi, Kenya
Shadia Clot, correspondent of the Sheikh in France
Waheed, Al Sadd travel agency, Qatar
Cécile and Karl, Emirates Airlines, Paris

SOUTH AFRICA
SATOUR, Ms. Salomone
South African Airways, Jean-Philippe de Ravel
Victoria Junction, Victoria Junction Hotel

SPAIN
His Excellency Jesus Ezquerra, Spanish ambassador to UNESCO
Club Meds of Don Miguel, Cadaquès, Porto Petro, and Ibiza
Canaries: Tomás Azcárate y Bang, Viceconsejería de Medio Ambiente
Fernando Clavijo, Protección Civil de las Islas Canarias
Jean-Pierre Sauvage and Gérard de Bercegol, IBERIA
Elena Valdés and Marie Mar, Spanish Tourism Office
Basque Country: President's Office of the Basque Government
Zuperia Bingen, director, Concha Dorronsoro and Nerea Antia, Press and Communication department of the President's Office, Basque Government
Juan Carlos Aguirre Bilbao, chief of the helicopter unit of Basque police force (Ertzaintza)

THAILAND
Royal Forest Department, Viroj Pimanrojnagool, Pramote Kasempsap, Tawee Nootong, Amon Achapet
NTC Intergroup Ltd., Ruhn Phiama
Pascale Baret, Thai Airways
Thai National Tourism Office, Juthaporn Rerngronasa, Ms. Watcharee, Lucien Blacher, Satit Nilwong, and Busatit Palacheewa
Fujifilm Bangkok, Mr. Supoj
Club Med of Phuket

TUNISIA
President Zinet Abdine Ben Ali
Office of the President of the Republic, Abdelwahad Abdallah and Haj Ali
Air Force, Laouina base, Colonel Mustafa Hermi
Tunisian embassy in Paris, His Excellency Mr. Bousnina, ambassador, and Mohamed Fendri
Tunisian National Tourism Office, Raouf Jomni and Mamoud Khaznadar
Editions Cérès, Mohamed and Karim Ben Smail
The Residence Hotel, Jean-Pierre Auriol
Basma-Hotel Club Paladien, Laurent Chauvin
Meteorological Center, Tunis, Mohammed Allouche

TURKEY
Turkish Airlines, Bulent Demirçi, former director, and Nasan Erol, press
Mach'Air Helicopters, Ali Izmet Oztürk, Seçal Sahin, Karatas Gulsah
General Aviation, Vedat Seyhan and Mr. Faruk, pilot
Club Meds of Bodrum, Kusadasi, Palmiye, Kemer, Foça

UKRAINE
Alexandre Demianyuk, UNESCO secretary general
A. V. Grebenyuk, administrative director of the Chernobyl exclusion zone
Rima Kiselitza, attaché at Chornobylinterinform

UNITED KINGDOM
England: Aeromega and Mike Burns, pilot
David Linley
Philippe Achache
Environment Agency, Bob Davidson and David Palmer
Press Office of Buckingham Palace
Scotland: Paula O'Farrel and Doug Allsop of Total Oil Marine, Aberdeen
Iain Grindlay and Rode de Lothian Helicopters Ltd., Edinburgh

UNITED STATES
Alaska: Philippe Bourseiller; Yves Carmagnole, pilot
Wyoming: Yellowstone National Park, Marsha Karle and Stacey Churchwell
Utah: Classic Helicopters
Montana: Carisch Helicopters, Mike Carisch
California: Robin Petgrave of Bravo Helicopters, Los Angeles, and pilots Akiko K. Jones and Dennis Smith; Fred London, Torrance Cornerstone Elementary School
Nevada: John Sullivan and pilots Aaron Wainman and Matt Evans, Sundance Helicopters, Las Vegas
Louisiana: Suwest Helicopters and Steve Eckhardt
Arizona: Southwest Helicopters and Jim McPhail
New York: Liberty Helicopters and Daniel Veranazza; Mike Renz, Analar Helicopters; John Tauranac
Florida: Rick Cook, Everglades National Park; Rick and Todd, Bulldog Helicopters in Orlando; Chuck and Diana, Biscayne Helicopters, Miami; Club Med in Sand Piper

UZBEKISTAN
Uzbekistan Embassy in Paris, His Excellency Mr. Mamagonov, ambassador, and Djoura Dekhanov, first secretary
His Excellency Jean Claude Richard, French ambassador in Uzbekistan, and Jean Pierre Messiant, first secretary
René Cagnat and Natacha
Vincent Fourniau and Bruno Chauvel, Institut Français d'Etudes sur l'Asie Centrale (IFEAC)

VENEZUELA
Centro de Estudios y Desarrollo, Nelson Prato Barbosa
Intercontinental Hotels
Ultramar Express
Lagoven
Imparques
ICARO, Luis Gonzales

We would also like to thank the companies that allowed us to fly on the basis of orders or exchanges:

AEROSPATIALE, Patrice Kreis, Roger Benuigui, and Cotinaud
AOM, Françoise Dubois-Siegmund, Felicia Boisne-Noc, Christophe Cachera
CANON, Service Pro
CLUB MED, Philippe Bourguignon, Henri de Bodinat, Sylvie Bourgeois, Preben Vestdam, Christian Thévenet
DIA SERVICES, Bernard Crepin
FONDATION TOTAL, Yves le Goff and his assistant, Nathalie Guillerme
JANJAC, Jacques and Olivier Bigot, Jean-François Bardy, and Michel Viard
KONICA, Dominique Brugière
METEO FRANCE, Mr. Foidart, Marie-Claire Rullière, Alain Mazoyer, and all of the suppliers
RUSH LABO, Denis Cuisy, Philippe Ioli, Christian Barreteau, and all of our friends in the lab
WORLD ECONOMIC FORUM of Davos, Dr. Klaus Schwab, Maryse Zwick

"Earth from Above" team, Altitude agency:

Photo assistants:
Franck Charel and Françoise Jacquot, who followed the entire project,
and all those who took part, Tristan Carné, Christophe Daguet, Stefan Christiansen,
Pierre Cornevin, Olivier Jardon, Olivier Looren, Marc Lavaud, Franck Lechenet,
Antonio López Palazuelo, Stéphane Rabaud, Jean-Paul Thomas

Coordination office:
Production coordination: Hélène de Bonis
Editorial coordination: Françoise Le Roch'Briquet
Exhibition coordination: Catherine Arthus-Bertrand
Production team: Antoine Verdet, Catherine Quilichini, Gloria-Céleste Raad for Russia,
Zhu Xiao Lin for China
Editing: Judith Klein, Hugues Demeude and PRODIG, geographic laboratory,
Marie-Françoise Courel, Lydie Goeldner, Frédéric Bertrand
Illustration documentation: Isabelle Lechenet, Florence Frutoso, Claire Portaluppi

Yann Arthus-Bertrand also wishes to thank his friend Hervé de La Martinière and the entire team
who worked on the book, particularly Benoit Nacci, artistic director, for his graceful support,
Carole Daprey, Marianne Lassandro, Christel Durantin, Amaëlle Génot, Marie-Hélène Lafin,
Jeanne Castoriano. And thank you to Quadrilaser, Kapp-Lahure-Jombar,
and SIRC for the printing and binding.

NEAR MAR DEL PLATA,
Buenos Aires, Argentina

Previous spread:
CRYSTALLINE FORMATION
ON LAKE MAGADI,
Kenya

All of the photographs were taken with Fuji VELVIA film (50 ASA).
Yann Arthus-Bertrand worked primarily with CANON EOS 1N cameras and lenses.
Photographs were also taken with PENTAX 640.

The aerial photographs of Yann Arthus-Bertrand are distributed by the Altitude agency in Paris:
30, rue des Favorites, 75015 Paris, France; e-mail: altitude@club-internet.fr
www.yannarthusbertrand.com

Printed in France